Parenti
different patn

Edited by Louisa Stanley
BA (Hons) QTS

Copyright Louisa Stanley 2024

Individual authors hold the rights to their own stories. Please do not reproduce any story without the author's permission. All information is correct as of May 2024.

Printed using Amazon KDP

Foreword
By Ian Caldwell (Menphys CEO)

"Every parent's journey with their child or children is unique. I'm so delighted that Louisa has brought the stories of so many families of children with complex needs into one place. Heart wrenching and humbling on the one hand but up-lifting on the other.

The stories are told with real honesty, from the heart. They share with us the heartache and sadness for what might have been. They also share the difficulties families have navigating the world with their child in trying to access the right support to enable their child to live the fullest life possible.

Whilst these stories will resonate with parents of children with complex needs, they will also resonate with everyone who has a child of their own. The unconditional love and the determination to give their child the best life possible.

The stories don't linger on dashed hopes and dreams that may not come; the stories are also full of joy. They show the true love of a parent for their child and of a child for their parent. They show how these special children make a telling and positive impact on everyone around them."

Contents

Introduction	page 6
A collection of poems by Steven Russell	page 8
Riding the rollercoaster by Louisa Stanley	page 18
Life with my Ausome son Oscar by Rebecca Hughes	page 27
Hermione: The little girl we gained by Helen Topham	page 31
Our special family by Paige Lines	page 37
Our lion, Arselan by Nida Zuberi	page 41
Grief – Grey compromise – poem by Nida Zuberi	page 48
'Keep going… you don't know what the future holds' by Mandy Harris	page 49
Not quite what I bargained for by Kelly anne Smith	page 53
Undiagnosed but not uncomplicated by Jasmin Manley	page 58
Our little miracle by Rachael Smith	page 63
Oh, the things I've learnt by Alison Hunter-Lehman	page 78
Our expectations vs reality- wouldn't change them for the world but I'd love to change the world for them by Sam Broughton	page 85
Our journey of courage by Natalie Greenall	page 90
'I don't know how you do it, you're amazing!' by Tina Fox	page 93
Gorgeous George by Aimee Meggitt	page 106

Be careful what you don't wish for by Rosie Naqvi-Dufty — page 110

Embracing a future we never expected by Judith Corry — page 116

Mummy knows best by Kathryn Anne Sankey (Marshall) — page 123

Living in a whirlwind by Jenni Jolly — page 127

Our SonShine by Mary Liquorish (Mazz) — page 135

"DUCHENNE" IS NOT HIS NAME! –
poem by Mary Liquorish (Mazz) — page 140

More than a statistic by Nichola Kerr — page 143

Misunderstood by Eleanor Wheatley — page 150

DDX3X: Our journey to diagnosis and beyond by Maria Poole — page 158

Why me? Well my dear, why not? By Fiona Williams — page 163

Our family's journey with Sanfilippo by Natasha Clarke — page 167

George's ASD rollercoaster by Holly Provost — page 172

Nenna's song – A Fairytale in 3 parts by Paul Arvidson — page 178

Final words by Louisa Stanley — page 187

Glossary — page 188

Support directory — page 189

Introduction

This book is a collection of inspiring stories and poems from the hearts of parents with children who have complex needs. As a parent of a child with Special Educational Needs and Disabilities (SEND), I fully understand both the challenges and rewards that our children bring to our lives. Many of us have been thrown into a new world, with no guidebook or signposts to support networks. We can often feel frustrated, alone and unheard. Here, we are given a voice, a chance to show the world our journeys; an opportunity to show how amazing, brave and strong our special children are.

The purpose of this book is also to provide support to other families who find themselves on this journey – you are not alone!

I wish to thank all co-authors for being so brave and honest in sharing your journeys and for finding the time to get your stories into words. Although I have changed spelling and punctuation, all the words are those of the individual authors. Most of the authors do not know each other, but the themes running through are so similar.

Throughout the collaboration of this book, I have felt guided by my late Grandad, Ray Wood. He is an inspiration to me in so many ways. He was awarded the MBE on 12th June 1993 for services to Menphys Playgroup, where he organised activities and transport for families with disabled children. I hope that he is proud of me. He has been in my thoughts in every stage of this book so it was important for me to mention him.

Sadly, he died in 2020, when Anna was 4. We never spoke about her diagnosis. He never treated her any differently. He accepted her for who she is, and I'm so pleased that they got to meet each other - they certainly had a very special bond. I come from a very loving family who continue to live life with my Grandad's positivity and strength. I feel very lucky to have this wonderful support around us. A particular thanks has to go to my AMAZING parents who have given me the strength and encouragement to be the person that I am today.

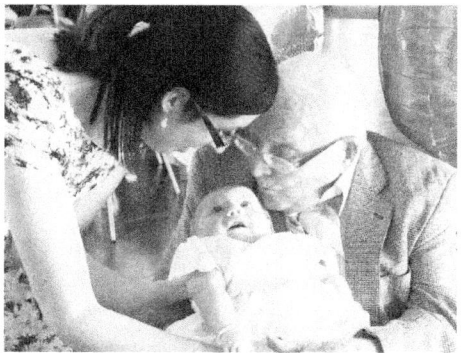

You will find a glossary and contact details for useful charities and organisations at the back of the book and if you resonate with any of the stories or poems featured, you can contact many of the authors in the Facebook group 'Parenting on a different path.' Together we can make a difference. The world needs to change. Our children deserve to experience the same opportunities as neurotypical children and I will continue to fight for inclusion and equal opportunities for all.
Louisa.

A collection of poems by Steven Russell

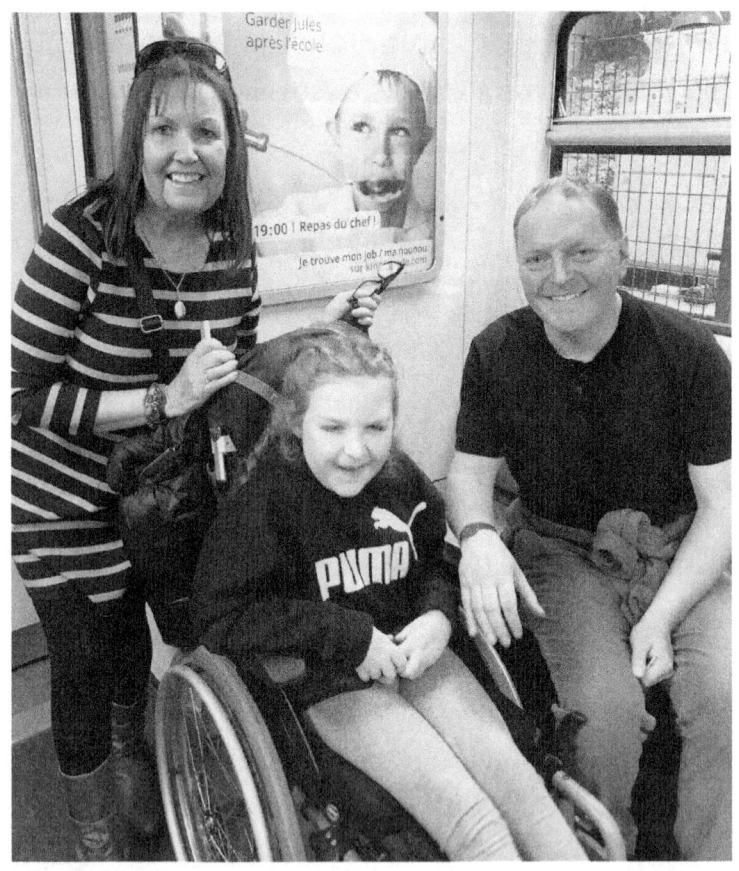

Steven and June Russell's daughter, Maia Russell, was born 12/12/05 with double chromosome abnormality. She is totally dependent on someone for every aspect of daily living. She is Nonverbal and a full-time wheelchair user (can weight bear to transfer). Despite all her difficulties, she is the happiest, smiliest little girl. Steven states "She inspired me to start writing poetry for the first time since school over 40 years ago. Just by watching her some days, verses come to my head and I write them on my phone, sometimes in as little as 15 mins. Once it's done it's done and I don't change anything as it's written just as it comes to me."

Roll up for the magical mystery ride

Roll up for the magical mystery ride

One of the first things you realise when you start the additional needs journey is you no longer take the regular route.

This has been replaced by a new route.

A route that takes you to places you have never been before.

A route that at first seems frightening and fills you with fear and trepidation but after a short while you realise is full of beautiful views and experiences. Yes this is the scenic route.

To complete this new journey you will board the magical mystery bus.

At first the bus is full and bustling with all the people you know and you set off full of hope and enthusiasm for the journey.

As the bus sets off down the road it makes a sudden stop. People are getting off and you wonder what's happening.

"Sorry," they say "We caught the wrong bus, this journey is not for us - we have another bus we need to take."

With a little sadness you wish them well and wave them good-bye.

The bus carries on and for a while, all seems settled and good.

Suddenly the bus stops again more people are getting off.

"Sorry," they say, "We enjoyed the short trip but it's not really for us we are going to catch another bus that's more our style."

As you wave them goodbye you notice people are getting on.

"Hi," they say, "We took the wrong bus before, this seems to be the right one for us now."

You welcome them on and the bus pulls away.

As the journey continues, more and more people are getting off and some new people are getting on.

This continues for a few stops but then you start to realise more people are getting off and less getting on. Things seemed to have settled now but occasionally the bus stops to let people off.

Although you feel a little sadness that many people have now left the bus you have a little smile to yourself as you watch the people who joined the bus.

They are all giving advice on how to enjoy the journey and sharing new maps with each other. You sometimes wonder why the bus is going so slowly but then you witness some of the most beautiful views that you have ever seen and realise you just need more time to take it all in.

As the bus carries on, you realise there are a lot of empty seats but also realise the ones that are taken are by people who are most definitely on the same journey. They are the ones you are meant to be with, to share this magical mystery ride.

As the bus carries on some of the people that got off earlier get back on and ride a few stops. As they leave they say how much they enjoyed the ride and will definitely look to rejoin at some point.

And that's ok because this is not their journey they have their own to take, but just traveling a short ride with you is fine and you look forward to the next time.

Sometimes when you are able you even join their journey for a few stops.

You always end up back on your own journey though.

It maybe slower paced but it's your journey and it's just how you like it. xx

I Wonder

I wonder what you'd tell us, I wonder what you'd say
If you could only find the words, if only for one day

Would you tell us that you're happy, would you tell us that your glad
That we had both been chosen to be your Mum and Dad

I know words are not everything, and you don't have a choice
But every day I send a prayer, just to hear your voice

I hear you talking in my dreams, and sometimes see you walk
But it only makes it twice as hard when I wake and you can't talk

I know your life is precious and I must realise
That every word you need to say is in your wide bright eyes.
They're in your touch and in your smile and everything you do
Don't ever change a single thing, just keep on being you.

Dear friend...

This poem relates to the difficulty of keeping friends when your life becomes completely different to theirs.

Dear Friend....

We hope one day you'll understand

This journey that we never planned

How do you cope, you used to say

We have to, there's no other way

The struggles can be so intense

Our future plans can make no sense

We only live from day to day

To find a normal life we pray

How can we help we sometimes hear

Just let us know that you are near

A text, a message on our phone

Will let us know we're not alone

A cancelled day that we had planned

We only hope you understand

We'll try again things will be fine

If only we can find the time

Our life has changed in many ways

We said goodbye to care free days

A little girl depends on me

She must come first I hope you see

We didn't mean to leave so long

Our friendship that had been so strong

There's faults both sides I can't pretend

But soon we'll meet again....Dear Friend

I Cried

This one's from my own personal experience of thinking I need to be extra strong for everyone else and hiding my feelings.

I Cried

I cried in the kitchen when everyone had gone.

I cried in the car listening to our song.

I cried in the bedroom when no one else was near

I cried in the garden where only birds could hear

I cried while out walking standing all alone

I cried in the sitting room scrolling on my phone

I cry almost everyday, as I watch you struggle on

But when I see you smiling it's then the tears are gone.

Why

That feeling in the beginning when you don't understand why but realise our kids are a blessing.

Why her, why us?

Why did you throw us under a bus?

Why did you curse us and cause us such pain?

Did it make you feel good, what did you gain?

Did we do something wrong, that we don't understand?

Or was this always just part of your plan?

To take ordinary people and turn them around

And share with the world this pure love that they found

It's taken a while but I now realise

Something so special in front of my eyes

It took me some time to figure it out

But now I can see, without any doubt

A greater love, I'll never find

Forgive me Lord, for being so blind

She's not a curse, I now realise

But a blessing that came, in a perfect disguise

She changed our lives, for ever it's true

This Special gift that came straight from you

So every day we'll keep doing our best

And never forget we've been truly blessed.

<u>We have to carry it</u>

This one's about the fear of the future and not knowing what's the best outcome. Our daughter dying first or us and who would look after her. Sorry it's a bit morbid but it's a subject we all think about. We carry our fears around with us everyday

We have to carry it

around in our hearts and our souls everyday

And it's tearing us down but there's no other way

We have to carry it

and it's breaking my heart, I ain't gonna lie,

Who's gonna care for you after we die

We have to carry it

and it's tying me up with knots in my chest

Who goes first what's for the best?

We have to carry it

If I go first will you know where I've went

If you go first my whole life will be spent

We have to carry it

sometimes we can't sleep as it weighs on our mind

And an easy solution we know we won't find

We carry the heartache for all of our days

Not knowing the best way for when we pass ways

But all we can do is keeping giving our best

And remember each day that we've been truly blessed

Girl in a chair

Girl in a chair. Did you look did you stare?

Did you pass time of day? Did you hurry away?

Did you stop for a while? Did you take in her smile?

Did you look in her eyes? Did you then realise?

That the girl who's sitting there, is so much more than a Girl in a chair.

Just A Girl

Just a girl no more no less

Just a girl trying her best

Giving it all in your own special way

Giving us sunshine on a dark cloudy day

Raising a smile from all who you see

Raising belief from deep inside me

Fighting each day with what comes along

Fighting to show them how much you belong

Making us realise this life is to live

Making us blessed with the love that you give

Just a girl no more no less

Just a girl trying her best

Superhuman

When people say you're superhuman but you know you're just an everyday person having to do a superhuman job for your child.

They say you're super human, but I know that you're not

You're just another Mummy (Daddy) giving all you've got

No Superhuman powers just giving from the heart

And loving me with all you have until the day we part

Each day I see you struggle on but never do complain

You'll wake again tomorrow and do it all again

They ask you how you manage to make it through each day

You tell them you don't have a choice this is the only way

I wish that I could tell you how much you mean to me

But, I don't have the spoken word just hope that you can see.

They say that special parents are gifted kids like me

But you are human just like them if only they could see

You crash, you burn, you fall, you cry

You rise again and don't ask why

They say you're super human, but I know that you're not

You're my amazing Mummy (Daddy) giving all you've got. Xx

Riding the rollercoaster

(The ups and downs... sometimes loving the thrills and sometimes you just want to get off!)

By Louisa Stanley

Louisa Stanley is a Mum, teacher, and carer for her daughter, Anna, who has Pitt Hopkins Syndrome. This is a mutation of the TCF4 gene and affects all parts of her development. It affects only 4 in a million worldwide. Louisa lives with her partner and daughter in Leicestershire, England. She now runs Believe and Bloom Education where she supports children with emotional and educational needs. If you are interested in support for your child you can find me on facebook: https://www.facebook.com/BelieveandBloom, or visit my website: https://believe-and-bloom.newzenler.com/

Riding the rollercoaster
(The ups and downs...sometimes loving the thrills and sometimes you just want to get off!)

When growing up, I always longed to be a Mum but had a feeling in the back of my head that it would never happen. So, imagine my excitement when in 2015 I found out that I was pregnant. I loved being pregnant and I actually felt really well throughout. Everything seemed to be going smoothly until the 12 week scan. We went along with no concerns to be told that something was very wrong; the consultant soon came in and whisked me away for further tests. They concluded that the baby had Cystic Hygroma (a build up of fluid around the body) that would most likely grow, and I would suffer a miscarriage. Consequently, the following few months were very tough, having regular scans but miraculously, the fluid gradually decreased and a miracle had happened - all now seemed fine but they were a little concerned about her size.

I was induced at 37 weeks thinking everything was normal. Unfortunately, after being monitored so thoroughly throughout the pregnancy, we felt incredibly disappointed in the lack of care in hospital. This resulted in our precious daughter, Anna, being born face first, all battered and bruised and she had to be taken to the neonatal unit due to breathing difficulties. She was only 4lb 8oz so she also needed to put on weight. When questioning the lack of attention we were given, we were told that it was our own fault for having a baby in October, one of the busiest months and they were short staffed! The midwife may have been joking but when my daughter was at risk, this was not a time for humour.

The rollercoaster was well and truly underway by this stage. To finally have the baby I had always longed for in my arms, for her to then be taken away was heartbreaking. Fortunately, I was able to stay in the hospital and I had my own room so I was able to go up and visit her in the early hours when I felt alone. This was actually a really special time – I have fond memories of creeping around the hospital in the middle of the night just to sit by her side. I just wanted to cuddle her but I couldn't – I just wanted to feed her but I couldn't – I just wanted to help her but I couldn't! This was a real waiting game – we had no idea whether she was going to stay for days, weeks or months and we daren't ask. It was hard to look around and see such poorly babies. Did we have the fight to get through this? We knew we had to be strong for Anna but little did we know that this was only the beginning of our bumpy journey through parenthood.

After 10 days in neonatal, Anna was deemed well enough to return home. Anna was a pretty good baby, she didn't cry much and she was quite content. Everything seemed perfect – we had our baby girl home and she was well and gaining weight nicely. Things were good – we started to go to every baby group around and we met some amazing friends. It didn't take me long to notice that Anna was different to all the other babies – at first I put it down to her being smaller and having to catch up, but then she wasn't meeting the milestones that other children were.

Another memory that is particularly clear is the day Anna started nursery. Most parents dread their children crying as you walk away and leave them for the first time, but I longed for this... I wanted Anna to feel a connection and want me, but she showed no signs of separation anxiety at all. Was I a bad Mum for wanting her to cry? I was told that I should be pleased, but I knew something wasn't right. She didn't respond to the same stimuli, her body moved in different ways and she was unable to roll, or sit up. This was particularly noticeable in swimming, where she would lock her arms back and not put them in front. Luckily, we had a great Health Visitor who was very supportive and referred us to a Paediatrician.

At about 9 months old it was becoming clear that Anna had significant difficulties – we were told that it was likely that she had a syndrome but we may never find out what it was. This was heartbreaking and we went down various routes to get a diagnosis – thinking this would solve all our worries. During this time, we found great support through SWAN UK (Syndromes Without A Name – a support network, run by the charity Genetic Alliance) and we are still involved with them today. Eventually through analysing our bloods and comparing them to Anna's, a diagnosis was found when Anna was 3 and we were called in to see the geneticist. Anna had Pitt Hopkins Syndrome – a rare genetic syndrome affecting only approximately 4 in a million. To hear this, the rollercoaster came crashing down. I think in the back of my mind I was hoping that it was all a mistake and they'd got it wrong, but looking at the characteristics of the syndrome – it was Anna completely.

From this day onwards, we were thrown into a whole new world. Although we felt lucky to get some answers, there was a real element of grief. We went through (and still go through) various stages of denial, isolation, anger, depression and acceptance. It really was like grieving for the child that you no longer had – the expectations of how parenthood would be had completely changed. One of the hardest things was not to compare to other families, and even now that is so hard not to do. It takes a lot of energy and strength to bring the focus back to our family and the wonderful daughter that we have. Sometimes seeing other families with children running around doing what looks like normal activities can pull at the heartstrings. Looking back, in one Music group, the leader went around the circle and every child sang their name. When she got to Anna, I always sang her name for her. Normally this was fine. I had gotten used to it, but then one girl stood up in the middle of the circle and sang 'Twinkle, Twinkle' to the group; I just crumbled. I left the session and sat and sobbed in a side room. Luckily, a close friend was there with her child and she came through and just hugged me. That's all I needed… to feel supported. I can't remember what she said but I know that she helped reassure me that I wasn't alone.

I can be feeling absolutely fine and then something can trigger me and hit me like a tonne of bricks when I least expect it! I deal better with this now, but it still hurts.

It's fair to say that dealing with the diagnosis is an ongoing process and both Anna's Dad and I went through these stages at different points, which compounds the feelings. Dad just wanted to fix things and would forever be on Google searching for answers and cures. I couldn't go there. To me, as long as she is healthy and happy then that's who she is meant to be. We soon got involved with the Pitt Hopkins UK charity, and this helped us feel less alone on the journey.

The COVID pandemic in 2020 had a massive impact on our lives but it wasn't all bad. Anna loved her time at home with Mummy and Daddy and the weather was gorgeous so we spent a lot of time outdoors. But the lack of social contact led to anxiety for Anna and support from professionals was limited. Sadly. our wonderful Paediatrician also died during this time and we were put at the back of a long waiting list to see someone. During this time we managed to get involved with CAHMS which has been a great support. Finally, after several years of fighting, we are back with a Paediatrician and feel we are being cared for again.

It was during the pandemic that I started to re-evaluate my work. I had been a teacher for 20 years but spending time at home with Anna made me realise what she needed. At work, I had been put on an attendance and stress management plan rather than given support and understanding. How could I give myself to 32 kids a day, with very limited support and then spend only 20 minutes with Anna? I knew the balance wasn't right and, with my mental health suffering, I left the classroom in December 2021 and set up Believe and Bloom Education where I am now able to support children with their emotional and educational needs, mainly working with children who are struggling to access school. Many of these children have SEND or

SEMH needs and have been failed by the Education System. I now love my job and I have a much better work life balance.

Anna is now 8 and we have good times and tough times. It's true that the good times are really good, but the bad times are really tough. The simplest of things makes us so proud – like using 2 hands to hold a ball, engaging in eye contact, making a new sound, and walking with less support, but we do get some challenging behaviour due to her learning difficulties and lack of communication. One of the hardest things is that Anna is non verbal so she often uses challenging behaviour such as headbanging to demonstrate her needs This can be very distressing to watch. It's exhausting trying to guess what she needs... is she hungry? tired? frustrated? in pain? We are using Makaton and basic PECS cards as an alternative way to help her communicate. My favourite phrase at the moment is, 'It is what it is' and this helps us get through the tough times. We need to focus on what we can control and trust that things will be ok again. Anna has taught us so much.

We don't know what the future holds for Anna and this makes our days tough – will she ever walk independently? Will she be able to communicate? There are no answers – we just have to be patient and wait and see, taking each day at a time and not looking too far ahead. I have found myself constantly questioning decisions we make – sometimes we get it right and sometimes we get it very wrong! But I've learnt to deal with Mum guilt by reassuring myself that the fact I feel guilt means that I care and I am making decisions from the heart with the best intentions.

Despite the struggles and worries, Anna has defied the odds at all stages:

-We were warned that she probably wouldn't survive pregnancy....she did.

-We were told that she'd possibly need multiple operations at birth... she didn't.

-We were told she may never walk…. She has and continues to challenge this.

We are so unbelievably proud of her strength and determination.

Throughout our journey, one of the toughest things has been the views and comments of others. I have people regularly ask me 'What's wrong with her?' or 'Will she get better?' and one particular comment from a friend really hit hard. When talking about the possibility of having a second child, she looked me in the eyes and said 'Don't you want the chance to be a proper Mum?' Now it's fair to say I now see very little of this person as I am no less of a Mum, and Anna is no less of a daughter. I'm being the best Mum I can be – and adding this pressure didn't help my mental health at all.

I've had my battles with anxiety and depression long before Anna came along so I have learnt strategies to deal with them. One of the most helpful things for me was being referred to a social prescriber through our GP. She put me in touch with the Carer's Centre, Leicestershire who have supported me to this day.

Anna has a way of bringing the best out of people. She has a remarkable ability to make others smile and I believe she has been given to us for a reason – she demonstrates strength and determination and makes us appreciate the simplest of things in life. She has the most naughty and contagious laugh which lights up the room – you can't be sad when you're around a happy Anna. We often wonder if she knows more than we think.

We have been lucky to have found wonderful groups locally in Leicestershire that have provided support to us as parents and provide services for our children. (see support directory at the back of the book). One charity, Menphys, has always been part of my life. My Grandad was involved with Menphys from the beginning, organising transport, arranging holidays and a number of trips to Lourdes; he soon became chairman and in 1993 he was awarded an MBE for his services to supporting families with disabilities. My parents then met when volunteering there back in the seventies and now we access the support. It's strange how life turns out and goes full circle but we feel very comforted and blessed by this. He has definitely been my guide in the compilation of this book.

I feel blessed to be chosen to be Anna's Mum. As a teacher I feel more empowered and passionate about inclusion and celebrating differences. Also, without Anna we would never have met some of the amazing people that join us on this journey.... from amazing children, inspirational parents, such great charities and a select group of remarkable people that just understand. I actually have an imaginary 'gold book' which is a record of these 'special' people. Maybe a professional has gone out of their way to make you feel supported, a stranger has shown kindness towards us, or a friend who just 'gets it'. I've made so many special friends for life, that understand and don't judge us. In a world of struggles and negativity, Anna has allowed us to see the good in people and help us to make the world a better place.

I will continue to fight for a world of equality and inclusion and I am passionate about getting support to families in need. My advice is to pick your battles but we are our children's voices and we must be listened to. What I can say is to 'Be a lighthouse in other people's storms.' When you're in a good place, be there for others as you may need them when times get tough for you. The greatest support we have found is with fellow SEN families. I feel as if we are sailing in different boats in the same ocean, passing by and helping each other in times of need.

Unfortunately, in this current world, families like ours have to fight for everything! One of my biggest gripes, that I will continue to battle is for our children to have access to holiday clubs like neurotypical children without costing parents the earth! For a start, there is a real shortage of suitable provision. Locally, we are fortunate to have FTM dance and we get one session a week funded in the holidays. If we have to pay privately, why should such provision cost us so much more than a mainstream holiday club? I have brought this up with our local MP where I was told that all placements should be inclusive and open to all children. In reality this is not the case. Anna would not cope in a mainstream holiday club and staff would not have the skills or resources to cater for her needs. Surely in this day and age, these children should be entitled to more. Anna should have the same opportunities for play and social interaction as any other child.

To conclude, this roller coaster has definitely had its twists and turns and there's certainly more to come, but by staying strong and being honest with ourselves and others, we know we have an exciting future. I'm sure Anna will continue to amaze us and make us proud. Thank you to everyone who continues to support us on this thrilling rollercoaster ride.

Life with my *Ausome* Son Oscar

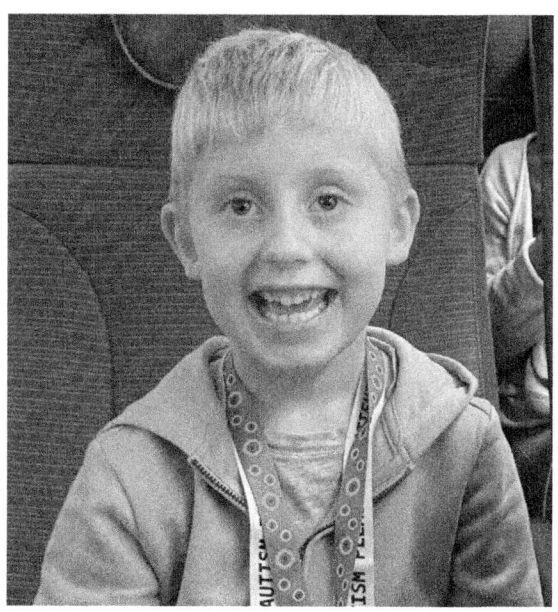

By Rebecca Hughes

Rebecca Hughes is a mother of two children. Her youngest, Oscar, was diagnosed with Autistic Spectrum Disorder at the age of 3. He is flourishing in his mainstream school in Leicestershire with the help of 1:1 teaching assistants.

Life with my *Ausome* Son Oscar

My son Oscar was diagnosed with Autistic Spectrum Disorder at the age of 3. He is now 6 and is settled in Year 2 at our local school in Leicestershire. It has been quite a journey raising a child with SEND after raising our daughter who met her developmental milestones.

My pregnancy was normal, apart from having to increase my Epilepsy medication as I gained weight. I booked in for an induction because of my health issues and it worked quickly, waters broke as expected and I was sent to the delivery suite. All was going fine until they realised that Oscar had become stuck, and many doctors and nurses had to come into the room. He wasn't breathing when he was born. They had to take him for a couple of tests to make sure that everything was ok, and I had to stay in the suite for several hours after giving birth until I was stable as I'd lost lots of blood. After a couple of days, we were able to go home.

In his very early life, I didn't really think that there was anything untoward. I just remember that he was a quiet baby (that could have been one of the red flags for Autism.) He hardly ever cried and was quite happy to let the world pass him by. At his 9 month check, he wasn't able to sit up properly in a high chair but the health visitors didn't pick up on anything- it's a tick box exercise.

In August 2019 when he was 2 ½, he started the local playgroup and there were assessments every so often about how the child was meeting his milestones. Oscar was typically falling around 18 months behind in terms of social interaction. He wasn't talking and would often spin around, which we now know was stimming for self regulation. I would also take Oscar to our local toddler groups but he often wouldn't play with the other children and preferred to be on his own.

In October 2019, I booked an appointment with the local GP to get Oscar referred to a paediatrician. I wanted to get everything in place before school. We were put on the waiting list. In the meantime, we found a private paediatrician at the Nuffield hospital in Leicester. He diagnosed Oscar in 6 sessions, way before the NHS appointment came through. He diagnosed him on the basis of delayed speech, obsessive behaviours and difficulties with social interaction. I went back to the playgroup and the staff there were brilliant in getting the ball rolling on a SEND support plan which was used to support him when he was 3 ½ at the local preschool. The next stage was applying for an Educational Health Care Plan (EHCP). We were granted this in March 2021 ready for school.

I wouldn't change Oscar for the world, but there have been difficult times. Once we had the diagnosis, we were partly relieved as we knew we could receive help, but didn't really know where to start. He has had an obsession with cables such as iPhone chargers since 2019. We have so many different electrical things plugged in at home. There aren't many 6 year olds who know the term HDMI or extension lead. In the summer holidays, we went to the cinema and what was quite a normal family day out, watching a family film, eating popcorn, ended in quite a stressful situation when he spied a phone shop on the way back to the car. What did he want? A phone charger! We were physically dragging him up to the car with him going redder and redder and screaming - most people would not have understood what was going on.

He is doing much better socially now but he knows when he needs his break out space. He plays really well with Reception aged children and loves role-play, such as preparing us meals from his pretend restaurant. He also enjoys dressing up, such as in his Batman costume at Halloween. At school, he takes part in Lunch Bunch, where he enjoys activities with a small group of children. He can get overwhelmed at times and ear defenders help him. Because his speech has developed now, he asks a lot of questions. It is particularly difficult on the way to school because he does not like me talking to another adult and will become more and more frustrated if I don't answer his questions straightaway and the answer has to be something he's happy with. The other day, Oscar suddenly started asking about the name of a previous teacher that he liked. His dad spent 15 minutes trying to think of the name, all the while with Oscar having a major meltdown. When Oscar finally remembered the name, he went back to being completely calm.

Oscar is starting to show a caring side. He cuddles his toy tiger in bed and says he loves me every night, which is the best thing ever. Oscar is definitely unique. A quote I really like about Autism is: 'There are no missing pieces. They fit together perfectly. They just make a different picture.' Oscar is just wired differently and I am sure he will accomplish great things in his own time.

Hermione: The little girl we gained

By Helen Topham

Helen Topham is a former English teacher, now full-time carer for her 5-year-old daughter Hermione, who has Down Syndrome. She writes a blog of their life entitled 'Our Gentle Hermione.' Down Syndrome is a genetic condition which occurs naturally at conception. An extra copy of chromosome 21 affects all aspects of development and can cause some health issues too. Helen lives with her husband Danny, her elder daughter Rose, Hermione and their little dog Woody in East Yorkshire, England.

Hermione: The little girl we gained

It's funny. I'm sitting here about to write our story, and I'm thinking about all the times I have had to write parental reports for Education, Health, Care Plans; DLA forms, blue badge applications and carer's assessments…you name it, I've written it.

All the times when I write what she can't do; what she struggles with; what impairments she has just to 'prove' that she deserves the support to help her thrive as a human being. I paint a picture of a little girl significantly behind her peers and I feel I betray her.

How wonderful that I am now able to paint a picture of a little girl who seeks the joy in life; who has likes and dislikes; who loves and is loved. Although this little girl is 'significantly behind her peers' and does indeed struggle with several aspects of life, she is, and always will be, our precious daughter.

Hermione was born in 2018; early at 36 weeks. I like to think she couldn't wait to challenge the world about the misconceptions of Down Syndrome/Trisomy 21. She was not going to conform to a set of characteristics in an outdated textbook.

I sailed naively through pregnancy. Eleven years earlier I had had another daughter, and I hadn't worried too much. It was not until the 20-week scan with Hermione that we had any inkling of Down Syndrome. The sonographer pressed hard on my stomach to get a better reading of the fluid level on the back of Hermione's neck (nuchal fold), and her eyes began to avoid mine. She handed my husband and I an alarming amount of scan pictures, and I think it was then that I began to feel a seed of something different happening to us.

We were told to come back later that day to try to get a better view of Hermione's nuchal fold, and so we ate breakfast in a local café and waited.

On our return, it was no longer the sonographer who attended us, but a consultant: a softly spoken Irish lady, with whom I placed all my trust. I appreciated her gentleness and let her mother me. I felt I was a child again: wide eyed, exposed and vulnerable.

We were taken to the Butterfly suite, the name emblazoned in calligraphy font on the door, and I glanced at the pristine white cups and saucers on the sideboard. Tea for sympathy. Tea for bads news. My heart was beating in my throat as I saw leaflets on the coffee table: Spina Bifada; Cerebral Palsy; Down Syndrome.

From the grave look on the consultant and specialist midwife's faces, it suggested this was bad. Really bad. Hermione had an increased nuchal fold. This could be a sign she has Down Syndrome; a chromosomal difference which means there is an extra copy of chromosome 21. This could cause developmental delay, some level of learning disability, a range of health problems and she may, well…look different.

We left the hospital clutching leaflets; barely speaking to one another: our hearts full with tears and information we could barely process. The air hung heavy with unsaid words, and we cried as we drove home. We spent the next hour torn between the beautiful, infectious excitement of our eleven-year-old finding out she was to have a sister, and trying to explain what Down Syndrome is and that her sister may be born with the condition.

We declined an amniocentesis which would have concluded for certain that our baby did, indeed, have Down Syndrome. We opted instead for a private, non-invasive blood test, which, in the present day I now have mixed feelings about, but, at the time, we were in a precarious position of wanting to prepare but also not wanting to risk losing our baby. The private test showed a very high chance of Hermione being born with Down Syndrome and so we spent the next sixteen weeks researching what it may or may not entail.

Our research was met with copious amounts of unflattering pictures and diagrams. The medical information became overwhelming and panicked me. I eventually came across a site called Positive About Down Syndrome (PADS) which tipped me towards a comforting thought: this might be okay.

I saw stories of children and adults living lives: getting jobs as bakers and gymnasts: obtaining degrees: having heart surgery but surviving and thriving. Having physiotherapy but walking; being tube-fed but staying alive and most importantly, being loved. The pristine white cups and leaflets in the Butterfly Room had painted a different picture. It suggested something had been lost, but what, in fact if something had been gained?

The connection I had with Hermione suddenly became a flickering light in a darkened room. She had not died. She was very much alive. Her scan pictures provided an anchor, and I studied them; only ever seeing a button nose and a little profile: our daughter: our baby.

The day after she was born, I came across a beautiful blog called 'Coraline and Us.' It was the story of a wonderful family raising an inspirational little girl with Down Syndrome called Coraline. To this day, her mum and I are still in touch, and she has encouraged and supported me to write my own blog.

Five years on, and I wish I could revisit my former self, and tell her what a joyful, meaningful life was awaiting her. Not that life wasn't meaningful before Hermione, but she has taught all our family a little something about deep love and patience; celebrating the milestones intensely when they arrive, and cherishing the extra dimension she brings to the world.

Are there challenges? Of course. I would never shy away from explaining the challenges we face. Hermione does have speech and language delay, which can be frustrating and upsetting for her and us. She requires lots of preparation when experiencing new situations. She is easily overwhelmed and struggles with some aspects of sensory processing. Walking came later and she is unaware of danger. But that doesn't mean she cannot learn.

When the longed for first few words tumbled from her mouth and she gained her autonomy, we brimmed over with pride. Walking, talking, holding a spoon or a pencil; learning to say her own name: everything is strived for. When she achieves these milestones, we celebrate tenfold.

Today, Hermione attends mainstream school. We are lucky that her school are very supportive, and her classmates have even learnt Makaton sign language to help communicate with Hermione and her with them. She teaches her peers something about kindness, patience and difference. Something I think the whole of society benefits from.

We tapped into our local support group, Downright Special, who are nothing short of spectacular. They run educational groups with specially trained early years teachers, who prepare and deliver specific resources for Hermione and her peers to learn how read, to form speech sounds, and have a deeper understanding of the world. Lifelong friendships were formed, and I can honestly say that some of the best people I was yet to meet were brought into my life because of having Hermione.

Learning that your baby is going to be different is overwhelming. I've felt it and I often still feel it. The extra work needed to navigate systems and local authorities alongside the day-to-day care of your child is incredibly hard work. But the rewards are something otherworldly. Hermione has enhanced our lives in ways we could never have imagined. The fierce love we feel for her has transformed all our values in life; our definitions of success and achievement and what it means to lead a fulfilling life.

Loving Hermione is a world away from the Butterfly Room. When she cups my face with her delicate little hands and looks at me; deep in the eyes, searching for who I am; we connect in a moment of shared understanding; that she is my daughter and I am her mum.

And as for looking different…Hermione does have beautiful, crystal blue almond-shaped eyes. She looks like her sister and her Daddy and she has the most infectious belly-laugh you could ever hope to hear in your life!

The meaning of the name Hermione is 'well-born' and we couldn't think of a more fitting name for a little girl who has intensely enriched our lives.

Related Blogs:

https://www.coralineandus.com

helenbielby.wixsite.com/ourgentlehermione

ourgentlehermione on Instagram and Facebook.

Our special family.

By Paige Lines

Paige Lines is a carer for her children Leo and Evelyn who both have Autism. Her daughter Evelyn and her husband Zak have a rare microdeletion called 15q 11.2 which causes learning difficulties and developmental delay and behavioural problems.

Paige wanted to share her story with others so that they never feel alone.

Our special family

I always wanted to be a mum. When I met my husband Zak, I just instantly fell in love; he is my best friend and we got married and started trying for our first baby. I fell pregnant and I was so excited to become a Mummy. The moment I saw the scan, I was so in love with my little baby. We found out we were having a baby boy and we could not be happier!

When Leo was first born, everything seemed perfectly normal, but once Leo reached the age of 1, we started to notice he was quite behind for his age and was not making any eye contact. My step dad was trying to take pictures of him in the garden and he could not get him to look at the camera. We started to notice Leo was starting to have meltdowns and becoming very frustrated, struggling to communicate his needs. I remember having a conversation with my Dad and my Mum. I asked them about my siblings and if they thought Leo was behind on his development and if there could be something wrong.

We made an appointment with our health visitor and she referred us to see Leo's paediatrician and they agreed that Leo could possibly be on the Autism Spectrum and sent us for the genetic testing. Leo's results were normal but we discovered Leo had Autism and was diagnosed by the age of 3 years old. Myself and Zak were in complete shock and had no idea how we were going to cope, as neither of us had any idea about Autism. I had to do a lot of research!

Leo is such an amazing little boy - so smart and funny! Things are not always easy; Leo has no sense of danger and he still struggles to communicate his needs and when he has meltdowns, he is incredibly strong and myself and Zak find it very difficult sometimes.

When Leo turned 5, we decided to try for baby number 2 …… What are the chances of Autism a second time round right?

We started trying for baby number 2 and I fell pregnant very quickly (a month later!) We were so excited but then Covid 19 hit and being pregnant in a pandemic was a challenge in itself! We had the first scan and I had to book a private one for Zak and Leo to attend as the NHS were very strict at the time and we were so overjoyed to see one healthy baby on the screen! We booked another private scan and found out that we were expecting a baby girl. I could not believe how lucky we were to get one of each! Leo was so excited to be a big brother.

Evelyn was born and we were so in love with her! Leo adjusted to his little sister so well I was so proud of him! Everything seemed perfect until we noticed Evelyn starting to progress backwards like Leo did. We started to have concerns, so we made an appointment for her to see the paediatrician and she had the genetic testing done and it turned out she has a rare microdeletion called 15q11.2 which causes learning difficulties, developmental delay and behaviour problems …… We were told its exactly like Autism but a medical condition. I was in shock and they asked for myself and Zak to get the test done as well so see if it was genetic and it turned out my husband Zak had the same deletion!

Zak always felt like he struggled all his life at school, communicating with others and having anxiety, so once we found out he had the same microdeletion as Evelyn, it started to make sense. I feel like we are a very special family and it just makes them more perfect in my eyes.

It is very hard sometimes for me to live in a household with special needs and at times I feel very overwhelmed, but I feel like it is so rewarding as well.

Leo is an amazing little boy - he has the most amazing laugh, it is so infectious it just makes you smile. Leo loves dinosaurs, superheroes and playing his Roblox game. Leo finds it very difficult to communicate and sometimes it causes him a lot of frustration; he has meltdowns and he tends to like his own space. He spends a lot of time in his bedroom just relaxing. He is brilliant with his little sister Evelyn - he loves to play with her and look after her.

Evelyn is a very sociable little girl - she is very affectionate and loves cuddles with Mummy and Daddy. She loves animals; her favourite is a cat (I think she would love a cat as a pet). She loves books and pretend play. Evelyn is starting to speak which is fantastic! But she struggles in other ways like with her eating habits. She doesn't like many foods and she will only drink out of a bottle at the moment. She also struggles to communicate and she gets very frustrated.

Leo and Evelyn are amazing children and I think they bring the best out in me. I think I was meant to have children with special needs as it makes me a better person and I love being their Mummy.

Our lion, Arsalan

By Nida Zuberi

Nida Zuberi is a mother, graphic designer/copywriter, carer and advocate for her 12-year-old son, Arsalan, who has Duchenne Muscular Dystrophy. This is a rare condition caused by an X-linked mutation on the Dystrophin Gene, affecting approximately 6 per 100,000 individuals primarily boys. Nida lives with her husband and her three children in London, United Kingdom.

Our lion, Arsalan

I heard the nurse's soothing voice encouraging me to push and my gynaecologist smiling back while I gave one last shove that took all my strength. My son came out perfect. He was born with ten fingers and ten toes, and he was gorgeous. He came into the world with a loud roar, and we named him Arsalan, the Turkish word for Lion. I remember it had taken me a long time to conceive after my first and I was ecstatic. My first was unplanned and unexpected but I was prepared this time and so happy throughout my pregnancy. This pregnancy was heavily anticipated and cherished; Arsalan's birth was such a celebration as my parents were there with me all the way.

While the first few months went by as they should, Arsalan started falling behind and didn't reach his milestones. He was first slow in sitting up, he started walking two months shy from his second birthday and he never jumped. My son's paediatrician chalked it up to pure laziness and as the growing feeling of unease ballooned into anxiety, I knew something was very wrong. Speech delay was apparent and as he grew, he wasn't cognitively at par with his peers.

Around 3 years of age, he wasn't interested in other children, and problems with communication only exacerbated his social awkwardness. He slowly started immersing himself in his own world, fixated on particular routines and sensitive to the sensory world around him.

We were initially living in Dubai, UAE back then and the doctors kept missing red flags and kept reassuring me that he would grow out of it. I wasn't getting any answers and my husband, feeling the same helplessness, pushed for a move to Houston, Texas, within his firm and we packed our lives and left.

Once settled, I hit the ground running even though I was seven months pregnant with my third child. I can't remember how many specialists we saw. One labelled Arsalan with cognitive delays. He was 4 by then. After delivering my daughter safely, I took a few months to recuperate and then booked another appointment with a Neurologist this time. I was more fixated with his cognition and behaviour and never in my wildest dreams did it ponder on me that it could be any other thing than him being on the Autism spectrum perhaps. I remember her looking at his enlarged calves. The hypertrophy of calves are initial recognisable symptoms, and she knew. Even with my insistence on an MRI, she just immediately ran a simple muscle test.

The reports came in. I remember that phone call, clear as day. His muscle enzyme CK levels were off the charts, his muscles were literally dying. A normal muscle CK level after a muscle injury is around 300 and his was 18,000. The doctor informed me that he had some form of Muscular Dystrophy. After visits to a specialist and genetic testing, he was diagnosed with the most severe form called Duchenne Muscular Dystrophy. It is an X linked mutation on the largest gene in the body, called the Dystrophin gene and I was a carrier and had given it to him. The Dystrophin gene helps keep the muscles of the body supple and working. With a mutation, my son wasn't producing full dystrophin and so his muscles would deteriorate over time. By age 10 or younger, he would lose his ability to walk, use of his pelvic muscles and then the ability to use his upper body, his shoulders, arms and his fingers. He would essentially be paralysed by late teens, trapped in a body that couldn't move. Unfortunately, lungs and heart are muscles too and they slowly give up as well and that's why it's 100 % fatal. There is no cure. Some die very young with a faster rate of progression and some in their late teens or twenties; very few live a bit longer. Since I had 2 X chromosomes, my healthy one kept me standing and alive, he had only one X chromosome and it would kill him. Furthermore, I was informed that speech and cognitive delays were part and parcel of the complication of the disease. "It's a rare condition," I heard the specialist say out loud. I will never forget her face at the Texas Children's Hospital, handing out a card about a support group. A support group for newly diagnosed parents with a terminally ill child. My son was slowly dying, and I was encouraged to attend. I never went.

My husband and I were in shock; I remember clutching on to hope and faith in God but as expected I was at a stage of complete denial or refusal to submit to the diagnosis, take it as you will. This was the catalyst to submerge myself into research. He wasn't dying on my watch, but above all, the guilt of leading a normal life and handing my son a death sentence is what literally drove me to action. I was going to fight. While researching about alleviating treatments, I stumbled upon a drug. It was in its final phase and was showing promise and it was up for FDA review and approval. It was a mutation specific drug that was tailor made for Arsalan. I became part of a sea of Duchenne parents writing letters to senators and governors urging them to get the FDA to approve, heavily supported by the phenomenal organisation PPMD (Parent Project Muscular Dystrophy). With harrowing testimonies from families, there was proof it was working. We waited, and the drug was eventually rejected. Shocked, I started looking elsewhere. The drug had been approved in the UK under the five-year managed access programme. We up and left the US.

Travelling and uprooting our lives yet again, and this time, landing in London, UK at the start of 2017. Arsalan was still walking albeit with a waddle but that was expected due to weakness. Admitted to Great Ormond Street Hospital care was a miracle and then the laborious process of getting him the drug, began. It wasn't a cure, but it would slow down the rapid progression of this disease. The day it arrived, on our doorstep in the month of June 2017, was a glorious sunny day. I remember my hands were shaking as I opened it. The search had started from Dubai. This was the hope in a box we were searching for. We had moved three different continents. God had opened impossible doors for us, even though it wasn't a cure, it was enough. This drug would keep my son walking for longer. We had truly come full circle.

It did help in a lot of ways, together with the standard steroid treatment, my son walked till his February birthday of 2020. When the Covid pandemic peaked, he slowly sat down, never taking a step forward again. It was truly a hard year. Before this we hadn't taken any time out to grieve. We were busy trying to move mountains for treatment, nothing else had meaning. It was difficult for the entire family but especially for him. It was the first sure sign of decline. We all took it hard. But we were truly inspired by our son's courage. He, out of all of us, took it in his stride. In fact, he had a sense of relief to be able to not worry about falling or getting tired. The wheelchair became a symbol of independence for him. His acceptance of it and embracing the inevitable awed us into accepting and moving away from the collective grief we all felt. My son is surely the strongest person I know. His grace and resilience throughout this journey have been a beacon of light for us.

Even though he takes these heavy transitions like a champ, it doesn't take away from how every year, every birthday is a year of decline. He calls himself an old man, dreams of having bionic legs and arms in the future. This does affect him mentally. Every loss of movement makes him less independent and not able to manage his sensory needs. It's a ticking time bomb, you don't know when the next phase of deterioration is going to manifest. Recently, he has developed contractures in his knees, due to the muscles deteriorating and now his knees remain bent, and he can't stretch his legs straight. The complications of this disease will never cease, not to forget how the rigidity and fixations of Autism adds to it all.

I once believed, despite how devastating this journey is that I would settle into the acceptance stage, but the more time passes, there is no respite forthcoming. The anticipatory grief is crippling, it has truly broken my heart into pieces. With a deformed fragmented heart, all taped up haphazardly, with all hopes and desires for his future shattered, I still fight on for his sake. If we give up, we know he will.

I've been advocating for him from day one, I'm a lioness, never wavering. Special Needs parents don't have a choice, we must fight for our children. So, I go on, making sure to find the right school for him after his additional diagnosis of Autism. Appealing to the Special Educational Needs (SEN) Tribunal when he was refused admission to a SEN high school. Making sure the provisions matched his needs in his Educational and Healthcare Plans. Educating school and the local council on this rare disease. Creating safeguarding protocols specific to his condition and so forth.

When your child has an all-encompassing illness and you have files and files on his entire history of it, your only option is to push forward. It's a rotating wheel of physiotherapy, occupational therapy, speech and language therapy, neurologist appointments, pulmonary function, heart medication, steroid side effects, bone density scans, blood tests etc. If I even pause for a minute to think, it leads me down to a path of dread, grief and immense pain, so I trudge on.

Despite all the heartache, I remember, my husband and I promised each other that we wouldn't transfer our anger and grief into the everyday functioning of our family. So right after his diagnosis, we travelled the length and breadth of the United States. We took him to Disneyland, Universal Studios and Legoland there as well as several times in the UK. We want him to experience it all before the disease gets the better of him. We've taken long trips around the UK, always making sure we choose all the accessibility routes and excursions. Wherever we go and whatever we do, we do all of it together. We go bowling, we go to restaurants, museums and to the Cinema. We create a cocoon of normalcy as much as we can. Life needs to be celebrated with whatever hurdles or limitations it throws at us, this holds especially true after the Covid pandemic. Grief is always lurking, but we've adjusted ourselves to this way of thinking and living. Mark my word, it is not easy, it is the hardest thing I've ever done, smiled while my heart was breaking. But optimism and this deliberate sense of normalcy helps my son take his sudden loss of mobility with greater resilience. He gets to embrace and enjoy more of the love and time we have for him. The love is in the time we spend together at home or anywhere we go. It is in the smiles and hugs that we give each other because hugs are precious. As his disease has progressed, it is getting more difficult for him to raise his arms, so we smile, we laugh, we hug and dance and we don't waste a single opportunity with our beautiful son.

We are never promised tomorrow. We know this journey is paved with heartache, but we won't let it break us as a family and let despair take over because this disease has taken a lot away from us, and we refuse to let it take more.

Grief- Grey Compromise
A poem by Nida Zuberi

Sometimes the weight of it all gets so heavy on your shoulders that day by day you feel your head exploding from the mere thought of it. You try not thinking about it but it's there, always there looming like a goblin on your back, never letting you walk straight into the light. Slowly spreading a greyish hue, seeping into all that is colourful. You try, you try sweeping it away, but it creeps back into the vibrancy of your life.

Sometimes you let it win and sometimes you fight for just a day of illumination by feigning amnesia disallowing it control, control over your slight existence. This is what a vicious cycle of grief feels like. It's always there, waiting, preparing, crippling. It never goes away. You live with it.

Then eventually defeated, you pull a chair out for it to sit, to be still, allow it to linger but not spread. You don't want it painting your life's canvas, compromising it. Stay with me you say, live in my head but try not to interfere. You keep it calm, dose it with optimism. Tell yourself live in the moment. Live in the moment, of course, nurture what you have. But nothing lasts and grief isn't a disciplined pupil. You learn it the hard way.

Days go by, drenched in black with greys in your hair.

Darkness conquers, reigns supreme.

Grief constant, grey compromises.

'Keep going.... you don't know what the future holds.'

By Mandy Harris

Mandy is a Mum and carer to her 17-year-old daughter, Olivia, who has Cerebral Palsy and Autism. Olivia's care is split between her Dad and her Mum. Olivia lives In Huncote, Leicestershire. with her Dad 50% of the time and Mum 50% of the time. Olivia is an only child and a very bright, engaging, funny, beautiful young lady.

'Keep going.... you don't know what the future holds.'

My pregnancy was healthy; I ate all of the right things and exercised sensibly. With it being my first child, I wanted everything to be perfect, it was an exciting but also daunting time. Just like in the movies when you see women wobbling around with a large bump, getting excited about having a precious baby in their arms. Little did I know what was about to happen.

It was a long excruciating labour that ended in an emergency caesarean. My beautiful daughter was born needing resuscitation. She was quickly sent to the neonatal unit to be intubated. I didn't meet my baby until 4hrs later after giving birth. We were told that she wouldn't survive and if she did survive, she wouldn't be able to see, hear, walk or talk.

My whole world was turned upside down, how could this be? I was healthy; there were no genetic problems within either of our families. From that moment on, our life wasn't our own, we were drowned by visits from doctors, neonatologists, midwives and consultants all whilst being in hospital as I was quite ill from the amount of blood loss, which resulted in an infection.

I vividly remember a nurse coming into my room at 5 am, to tell me I needed to decide as to whether or not I was going to take my daughter to a hospice so she could pass away peacefully there. I remember being shown where the morgue was so I could plan my journey there with my newborn baby in my arms. I was numb, I couldn't believe this was happening, it wasn't how it was supposed to be. I became obsessed with checking her breathing and felt like I was in panic mode all of the time.

Was this the time my baby is going to take her last breath or will it be tomorrow?

To our amazement, our daughter kept on breathing and is still breathing to this day; she is now 16 and a half years old. She had a diagnosis of Cerebral Palsy at the age of 1 and Autism at the age of 9. I knew her life wouldn't be like others, but I never knew how life would be. If anything, Autism is more debilitating than Cerebral Palsy as she doesn't leave the house very often, only to go to college.

Our daughter is unable to walk, has little speech, and uses an electric wheelchair; she also uses a communication aid and Makaton to communicate. My daughter has the most incredible sense of humour and lights up any room with her beautiful smile. She has taught me many things such as determination and resilience. She has had to fight all of these years to keep surviving, to keep going no matter what hurdles she has in her way.

After a meeting with the hospital, they said 'It was just one of those things and there was nothing else they could do'. We contacted a solicitor as I knew something was wrong, I knew my baby should have been delivered quicker than she was. They confirmed there was no case. My gut instinct knew there were mistakes but most people around me said, 'It was just one of those things and to leave it'.

We visited a disability roadshow and my ex-husband noticed some chocolates on a stall, he quickly went over to take one. We had a good conversation with the solicitor at the stall and explained our story.

Moving forward 6 years later, we have just won the hospital negligence case. The NHS Trust admitted there were mistakes made and settled out of court.

Our daughter's life will never be what we hoped for, which is heartbreaking to see but at least she will now be financially secure for the rest of her life.

Not Quite What I Bargained For

By Kelly-anne Smith

Kelly-anne Smith is an Autism and Parent Support Advisor, Teacher and Mum to 4 neurodivergent children who lives in East Yorkshire. Following her own professional and personal journey with Autism and Neurodivergence, she established SENsational Life where she now provides online support to thousands of families. Please visit www.sensational-life.com to find out more.

Not Quite What I Bargained For

When you first find out that you're pregnant, you start to think about all the wonderful things that you are going to experience with bringing your child into the world and watching them grow up. No one tells you or prepares you for what parenthood actually looks like when your child is disabled; ultimately brought up in a world that's not set up for them to succeed with a society that isn't as understanding and accepting as you would like to think!

My parenting journey started, quite unexpectedly, in my final year of university in May 2001 and I didn't really have a clue what I was doing! All I did know was that my boyfriend at the time (now my husband) was going to be a great Dad and that my uni dissertation and baby were due on the same date!

Thankfully I submitted my dissertation early, as I found myself spending my final weeks of pregnancy on bed rest in hospital and attached to monitors due to high blood pressure and having excess fluid around my baby.

After being hooked up to a hormone drip, my eldest son, Callum, finally made an appearance 10 days after his due date and, whilst most new parents will say similar, that is when my life changed. I had no way of comprehending at the time just how much that would differ from other new Mums and all my preconceived expectations of parenthood.

As a first time Mum, I did everything 'by the book' – we got involved in various groups, sensory sessions, went to baby massage (where me and Callum got a shiny certificate for our efforts!) but when Callum was about 8 months old, I started to shy away from socialising and baby groups. I had very little to talk about with the other Mums as my child wasn't hitting any of the milestones that they were obviously proud of and excited to share. Despite expressing my concerns over Callum's development and being told by the health visitor (and to be honest anyone that would listen) that 'Everyone develops at different times', 'He's a boy, boys are lazy', being made to feel like a neurotic first time mum who was always panicking over the slightest thing; I knew something wasn't right.

When Callum turned 2, a whole host of professionals suddenly became involved and numerous amounts of tests started. We were given social workers, support staff at nursery, speech therapy, we had occupational therapy - there seemed no end to the people that were now a part of our lives. Despite having all these professionals involved, I never felt understood or supported fully, and 90% of the time I had no idea what was going on – who was referring us to who, and for what. Professionals didn't seem to be able to give me any real kind of answers about the 'next step' or the future; everything was just so overwhelming and isolating.

Callum was initially diagnosed with Global Development Delay and, whilst it was tough, it was being out in public that I found the most challenging and mentally draining. The looks people would give us, the judgemental comments and unwanted parenting tips we would get everywhere we went. "Will someone shut that kid up!" was one comment we had shouted at us across the street when Callum was having a particularly overwhelming day and making a noise. Along with this, I remember one man staring so much at Callum in his adapted disability buggy (which at this point had his younger sister attached to it too, in a seat that had to be custom made for us) that he actually walked into a lamp post – although that did give us a laugh!

As our family grew, and Callum got a sister and 2 brothers, a whole different set of difficulties started to emerge - but this time it was with me. Not only had Callum gone on to receive a diagnosis of Autism and severe learning disability, but also his siblings were surpassing him and actually helping me take care of him and of each other. I felt tremendously guilty. Guilty of trying to balance my teaching job with my caring responsibilities at home (I was not good at this at all!), guilty of needing to spend more time with Callum than with them, but most of all guilty for not being able to give them the childhood that I felt they should be experiencing.

As the years passed it become apparent that Callum's siblings also had their own difficulties, so with a new set of professionals involved in our lives, more appointments and meetings in addition to those for Callum and me trying to work, things finally snapped.

Not acknowledging my own support needs and feeling like a failure to my profession, my work colleagues and my family, I had a mental breakdown; I was signed off work with depression, placed on medication and underwent numerous counselling sessions.

I had no idea how I was going to come back from this and take care of my children in the way they all deserved and yet it was at this point that my life started to take another direction, one that would not only go on to support me and my family but also families just like mine! I realised that my biggest problem was that I never felt like I knew where to go for advice, to be told what support was available to me and my family or how to actually get it, my feeling of isolation and guilt came from not having an understanding and supportive network, so I made my own; SENsational Life!

All those years of appointments for my children, all the form filling, all the meetings, emails and phone calls making sure that the right kind of support was put in place, all of it was always focused on the negative. What they couldn't do, what they struggled with, how they were behaving differently to others, everything just seemed to highlight how, as if in some way, they weren't 'good enough'.

There was absolutely no balance!

Yes my children are neurodivergent, are disabled and have difficulties but they are also much more; they are funny and caring, they enjoy so many different things and they matter just as much as the next person.

My children, along with their difficulties, continue to bring me so much joy. They have taught me that it doesn't matter about the views that others have of you only the view you have of yourself. Happiness has to be a top priority regardless of what scary changes that might involve and you always need to do what works for you and your family, no matter what other families or society are doing or expect you to do. They have also given me the answers to a lot of questions as through their diagnoses has come the realisation of my own neurodivergence too; I feel very grateful to have all 4 of them in my life.

Callum is now 22yrs old, is a nonverbal communicator and needs a minimum of 1 to 1 care ratio at all times. As he's grown so has his list of diagnoses, his difficulties and ultimately the physical and mental demands placed upon us as a family to meet his needs. But what has also grown is the unwavering love, and determination to not only make sure we remain solution focused to all problems encountered, but also to do everything possible to ensure he gets all the support and understanding he will ever need to lead a fulfilled life.

Undiagnosed but not uncomplicated

By Jasmin Manley

Jasmin Manley is a 29-year-old self-employed payroll clerk, blogger and author. She is an ex police officer who left the force to care for her son Max who has complex disabilities as a result of a rare, undiagnosed genetic disorder. Max is Autistic with Learning Disabilities, Microcephaly, Hypotonia, Hyper mobility, Dysphagia and was also recently diagnosed with Oculocutaneous Albinism. Jasmin lives at home in Cheshire with her son Max.

Undiagnosed but not uncomplicated

There were no signs during my pregnancy that anything was amiss. I suffered with Hyperemesis Gravidarum which is basically extreme morning sickness and I struggled to stay nourished and hydrated throughout my pregnancy. I remember being 9 months pregnant and weighing just less than nine stone because I'd barely been able to keep any food or drink down since around 7 weeks gestation. During my pregnancy, we had the odd appointment where the midwife would be concerned about Max's growth but we'd be sent for a growth scan and everything would be fine.

When I was three days past my due date a scan showed that Max had barely any amniotic fluid left around him and I was booked in to be induced the following morning. Nothing proceeded naturally with my labour and my waters had to be broken manually. Max's heart rate was sporadic and caused a few concerns to the point where, at 24 hours post waters breaking, I was given an episiotomy to get him out urgently. He wasn't breathing when he was born but after what felt like a lifetime of the team rubbing and patting him, I heard his little cry. After this, I haemorrhaged so I don't remember much, but after a few days in hospital we were both given the all clear to go home and start our lives as a family of three.

Max was an extremely unsettled baby. He was jaundiced for the first 2-3 weeks of his life; he would vomit up every feed and sometimes the regurgitated milk would block his airway and he would stop breathing. He would scream for hours on end and was in and out of hospital a lot but nothing flagged any long-term health concerns.

He was delayed in all areas of development from birth but because he was our first child, we didn't realise. He was always a very floppy baby and couldn't hold his own head up until he was nearly six months old, didn't sit until he was one, started crawling at 18 months old and didn't walk until he was over two years of age. By this time however, we were starting to have concerns over his development and behaviour as he was completely non-verbal with very little understanding, constantly lining things up or throwing them and would self-harm by banging his head against the floor daily.

The health visitor came out to complete the "two year check" and that was the first time a professional had told us there was something going on with Max. She said he was severely delayed in all areas and was "red-flagging" for severe social and emotional impairments. She referred us to what felt like every professional on the planet – speech and language, physio, OT, audiology, orthoptics, paediatrics. It felt like overnight we'd gone from a happy-go-lucky family thinking our child was quirky and a little bit behind to fielding countless phone calls, attending appointments and assessments where each professional would tell us all the things that were wrong with our child.

This was probably the hardest time of mine and my partner's SEND parent journey but thankfully our health visitor referred us to a local charity called Ruby's Fund. It was set up by the parent of a child with complex disabilities as a place for SEND families to go and receive advice and support. They supported us massively throughout those early years and the friendships we forged are still strong even now four years later.

I struggled massively with guilt in the early years, believing that Max was the way he was because of my parenting or something I had done wrong during pregnancy. This wasn't helped by his nursery SENCO who repeatedly told me that he'd start talking if I read to him more or that he'd start eating if I stopped giving him his safe foods. "He'll eat if he's hungry enough," is a phrase that still haunts me to this day. It haunts me because I was naïve and actually listened to that advice. I stopped giving Max his safe foods and instead offered him healthy alternatives, any alternatives. He didn't eat anything for 24 hours and so we caved in and gave him his safe foods. He didn't eat despite being starving, because he wasn't spoilt or choosing not to eat, he was Autistic and physically couldn't eat the food I offered him. The guilt of that decision is something I still struggle with now but I also use it to stand my ground when I know professionals are giving me incorrect advice or trying to do things that aren't suitable for Max.

Now that Max is six years old, the challenges we face are somewhat different to those of the early years. Whilst he still has the same behavioural, social and communicative difficulties, he's now a lot bigger and stronger making it harder for me especially to deal with. He is also requiring more specialist equipment, the older he gets, like a wheelchair, bath lift, specialist bed etc. Before I had Max, I assumed that disabled children were given all the equipment they needed by the Council/Government - how blissfully ignorant I was. We have had to fight for every piece of equipment Max has, even the small things like orthotic boots. We've had to fill out reams of paperwork, attend assessments and have professionals come to our house to witness how much support Max needs in order to justify why he needs funding for equipment.

We have been bounced back and forth between the NHS and the council with both stating the other is responsible for providing said piece of equipment. It's physically and mentally draining having to fight for your child to have equipment that you don't even want in your home because it's another reminder of how different your life is to everyone else's, but that they need just to be as healthy and independent as possible.

On top of the parental guilt, the endless battle for equipment, the worry about school places, the DLA and EHCP applications and the actual responsibilities that come with being a parent carer, I also really struggle with the fact that Max's overall genetic condition remains undiagnosed. The reason why our lives have turned out this way, why my son will forever be reliant on other people, just isn't there. Despite his geneticist and paediatrician both being 99% certain he has a genetic disease, all tests have so far come back negative and so we are now in limbo, waiting for the day DNA research catches up to Max's body.

However, despite the difficulties, I wouldn't change my son for the world. He is beautifully unique, incredibly determined and his smile lights up every room he's in. Max has taught me to treasure each and every moment of life. Every tiny milestone is a celebration for us and it means we never take things for granted. He has taught me about courage and resilience and he fills me with a pride I will never, ever lose. He is my everything and I'm thankful for him every day.

Our Little Miracle

By Rachael Smith

Rachael is a wife and mother of two, her son James is 8 years old and her daughter Emily is 3 years old. She has a degree in Childhood Educational Studies and is passionate about helping people. She is currently James' full time carer; he has Lennox-Gastaut Syndrome and requires around the clock care.

Our Little Miracle

My journey started in 2015; we were delighted to learn that we were pregnant and expecting our first baby. We were more excited because as a child I was diagnosed with a rare form of kidney disease so we did not know if we could get pregnant. When we did get pregnant, we were so thankful. At the 16-week mark, we went for a private scan and learned we were having a baby boy, our James. It was amazing seeing James on the screen like that, he was moving about and kicking away. What amazing images we now had! I couldn't wait to welcome him into the world, our little miracle. I was induced at 36 weeks as my Kidney function was dangerously low. The birth was quick, easy and straight forward with no complications.

At 5 months old, James started to get unsettled, constantly cried and went off his feeds. Then, on the 7th May 2016, 111 got us an out of hours appointment in A&E at 11pm. The doctor gave James a thorough check, she noticed a rash on the back of his neck and told me it was a heat rash and viral infection, to go home and give him fluids and monitor him. I asked if the rash was suspicious, "Could it be Meningitis?" I asked.
"No, you are just a worried first-time mum," was the reply. I was so upset that she agreed to have him monitored for 4 hours; we were then discharged home at 4am. James slept for an hour; I went to check on him around 6am and he was laying on his back with rapid eye blinking and constant odd mouth smacking motions. I had never seen anything like it. He wasn't responding.
The ambulance arrived within 10 minutes; the paramedics walked in and said "He has Meningitis."
This can't be right, I asked if it was Meningitis only 7 hours ago. It is just a virus, isn't it?

James was given emergency seizure medication and placed on oxygen before being carried into the back of an ambulance and blue-lighted to hospital. I didn't realise it at the time, but this would be the first of many ambulance rides with James. The paramedics did their best to reassure us; they spoke kindly, told us to try not to worry, that we had done the right thing in getting James help quickly. She explained the various forms of seizures and how they are not all in the typical form of Tonic Clonics which are shown so often on the television. Tonic Clonic seizures are the only seizures I knew about at the time, I had no idea there were so many different forms!

We arrived at A&E and were taken straight into Resus and the room filled with professional bodies. It felt like an eternity, but also a blur. Then someone came out to us and took James up to Ward 11 where he deteriorated and ended up in CICU (Children's Intensive Care Unit). He was having constant seizures which required emergency medication to help him come out. This is known as Status Epilepticus, which is a medical emergency that if left untreated can lead to permanent brain damage or death. Due to the prolonged and consistent seizures, James then required oxygen, his O2 levels were dropping rapidly and went as low as 40 before help arrived. He needed constant monitoring.

He had many tests during this time, including a lumbar puncture test. I had to be taken out of the room during this test because I couldn't stop crying. James was peeled out of my arms, as my sobs were shaking his poor tiny body, and it was very, very important that he lay in the fetal position as still as possible to avoid spinal injury. But I couldn't bare to see him in pain, suffering and crying. What a mess.
At this point every nerve in my body was shattered, I could not stop shaking and crying.

Afterwards, once the Doctors had left and I was allowed back in to the room, I picked up my baby and I held onto him for hours. I sang every nursery rhyme that I knew and I rocked him until he was fast asleep. We comforted each other in those moments and I kept praying for strength and healing, that it would all be over soon and we would be told everything was ok, that we could go home and go back to normal. But that wasn't happening just yet; James was too poorly to go home. He needed around-the-clock care and medication to keep him alive.

James was having frequent and strong medications through a cannula so it was advised that he had a long line inserted, which would allow long-term medication to be given, but without the pain of collapsed veins and the constant need to reinsert new cannulas which caused distress to James. This was another indication that home was a long, long way away. Finally, the results were back; James was diagnosed officially as having a viral infection within his brain, known as Meningoencephalitis - this involves inflammation to the Meninges layers that cover the brain and spinal cord (Meningitis) and inflammation of the brain tissue (Encephalitis).

As the days went on, we came to the end of the second week in CICU and he was able to move back onto ward 11, all signs that he was getting his strength back. We were told that James's MRI (Magnetic Resonance Imaging) showed scarring widespread across his scans, meaning he had irreparable brain damage and would have learning difficulties and problems developing throughout his life.

Then, almost a month after being admitted, James was discharged home. We had regular monthly Occupational therapy and Physiotherapy appointments, as well as having a hearing specialist and a named Neurologist, who we could call at any time for advice. Our lives had changed overnight, we were now living with a disability, the situation was awful. James was left with Global Learning Delay, loss of skills and abilities, required daily physiotherapy at home and medication throughout the day to reduce his seizure activity. He still smiled and he still melted the heart of anyone who knew him. Our Prince.

But I was changed, I was worried about everything. I didn't trust myself; my confidence was gone. I feared all germs and if we were in contact with anyone that seemed ill in any way, I would have an anxiety attack. I would have to hide away and protect James; this left me with sleepless nights where I would just watch over him and look for any sign of an illness, any fever, any rash, any missed meal would cause me worry. It was hard for people to understand, my reactions appeared irrational. But in my head, I was hiding away from germs and trying to protect James. I stopped seeing people. I stopped going out and my social circle dramatically reduced. I was so alone.

A few weeks went by and then James started head dropping in clusters, so I recorded the episodes and went straight to my GP who told me to go to A&E immediately to see a Neurologist as he suspected James was having seizures again. After being admitted to hospital and having an emergency EEG (Electroencephalogram, small metal disks are connected to the head to measure electrical activity in the brain) it was discovered that James's Epilepsy had got worse and he was having Infantile Spasms, another form of Epilepsy! This particular form of Epilepsy typically presents itself in babies and is referred to as 'West Syndrome'. The Spasms caused James to head drop, eyes to roll backwards and for his body to stiffen and his arms and legs to open out wide and stiff, whilst his body bent forwards into himself. These episodes only lasted about 2 seconds, but would go on to form clusters. So, we were taught how to administer emergency Buccolam medication for if these clusters went on for more than 10 minutes. They usually happened when he was tired, just woken up, or was eating, we also noticed that excitement and pain increased the seizure activity.

These seizures caused James to forget how to sit up, roll over, weight bare and even open his hands. Things were getting tougher. He needed a lot of hospital admissions, especially when he was poorly, as his seizures were long, violent and frequent, needing the Buccolam to break the cycle. He also spent a week in August 2016 in hospital with tonsilitis. This all put a strain on my own body and I was also spending a lot of time between hospitals having various forms of treatment for my kidneys. It was really hard managing my own ill health and James's ill health too. Around this time, James started a course of Prednisolone Steroid treatment. It was hoped that this would cure his Epilepsy. The steroids helped, but it was only a short-term treatment plan, so as he was weaned off, the seizures started up again, in the form of Infantile Spasms, Drops and Vacant seizures.

During this time, we saw the light at the end of the tunnel, relief and hope. Then we watched it disappear as the seizures grew worse and worse again. It was very sad. In late November 2016, we thought James was exposed to someone who had the sickness and diarrhoea bug. He was showing symptoms, and then the next day he had a prolonged seizure and the Buccolam did not bring him out of it. We rushed him to A&E. There was a long queue of people. I pushed to the front and begged for help; they hurried us into Resus where once again the doctors flooded in and started emergency treatment. After a few days in hospital on strong intravenous antibiotics for suspected tonsilitis, it was decided James could go home, even though he still had a high temperature and an upset stomach. We were sent home with oral antibiotics and given open ward access in case he deteriorated. During the night I woke up to find James fitting and looking very hot; he was black in colour. I gave him Buccolam, called 999 and took his temperature - it was 40.1C. The paramedics took us into hospital again and doctors flooded in and the same specialist nurse who saw us 7 months earlier told us the same words again. 'He has Meningitis'.

All those memories came flooding back, leaving me paralysed with fear and breathless. Watching James over the next week fight for his life all over again in CICU aged just 11 months old was heart breaking. How can this be happening again? He went back onto the life-saving drugs, he had another lumbar puncture test and was back on the oxygen. He needed another long line inserting because his veins had shut down during the harsh antibiotic treatment and the shock his body was under. The doctors were also testing for Sepsis. So, James was put on a waiting list for surgery, making him nil by mouth.

He was having prolonged seizures that required emergency medication to be administered intravenously; Eventually James had a long line inserted into his groin area as he was made a priority for surgery and he had this removed as his leg had turned a blackish colour and it had caused dangerous swelling to the whole leg which ran the risk of amputation! Back into CICU he went. I noticed James no longer made vocal noises or made eye contact. A specialist eye Doctor took him for a test where it was discovered he wasn't responding as he should. Once he was stable, he had another MRI which showed the infection had damaged the visual cortex within the brain, making him blind. The infection had also left scarring to the speech part of the brain, making him non-verbal. His scans showed massive widespread scarring. This was devastating news.

Over the next few weeks, family came to visit him in hospital. My husband, Ashley's birthday had been and gone on the 7th December, then James' birthday was the 13th and Christmas day; special events we were celebrating whilst in hospital. James met the Leicester city football team and Leicester Tigers team and they both gave James signed gifts and happily took pictures with us and chatted. Santa even came to visit with lots of treats!

The nurses were amazing, they gave us information, reassured me over and over again, listened to my worries, cared for James and put us in touch with various professionals who would be able to help and support us once we got home. James was finally discharged on New Years Eve 2016. What a year! We had all been on a rollercoaster, emotions were flying around and on top of that our lives had been turned upside down. We had to learn new techniques for caring for James, for meeting his needs and to help him develop to his full potential. We were exhausted and I remember losing hope with each milestone he missed. I had started out with a determination that the doctors were mistaken; James would be alright if I just pushed him harder. If I just tried harder. But with each seizure he had, it took what little development we made away again.

I said goodbye to mainstream education, goodbye to him walking and having sleepovers at his friends' houses. There was one point when James could say 'Daddy' which was an amazing achievement, but after a non-breathing epileptic episode in 2021, he also lost the ability to do that.

We have adapted; it's exhausting, but it works. The bar has been lowered to a more practical level and we celebrate everything. Every smile, every hour spent in bed at night without a seizure, every attempt at joining in with his friends we celebrate it all. We go out when we can, and if we can't that is ok. There are no unrealistic demands, no pressures and very little stress. James is happy and loved and we make new memories every day.

Due to the two cases of Meningoencephalitis that James suffered, he has been left with Lennox Gastaut Syndrome (Secondary to West Syndrome). This consists of drug-resistant Epilepsy and a high risk of SUDEP (Sudden Unexpected Death in Epilepsy). The last few EEG's that James has had, shows a constant state of Epilepsy. His neurologist says it is one of the worst reports he has seen and there is very little that can be done. We just have to keep trying various medications and using his VNS (explained below) and by keeping his head protected from falls. The worry with drug-resistant Epilepsy and SUDEP is that James is in a constant state of Epilepsy and any one of the seizures could kill him; his brain will eventually be too tired to fight. This is terrifying, we could put him to bed and he may not wake up, he could go to school and not come home. This is a constant worry and one that we cannot prepare ourselves for.

He has a mixture of non-breathing episodes, Tonic, Tonic Clonic, Absence, Drop and Myoclonic seizures. James was able to have a Vagal Nerve Stimulator (VNS) fitted, this clever battery pack works in two ways, there is an auto stimulation working in the background and when James's heart rate drops or increases between his recommended settings, a stimulation is sent through the vagal nerve to tell the brain to stop the seizure. The second method is a magnet that any adult looking after James carries around with them and if they see James having a seizure then they can swipe the magnet across the battery within James's chest and that sends a 60 second stimulation to the brain. This has reduced the number of A&E trips as he doesn't require as many Buccolam rescues and the battery lasts between 3 and 5 years, so surgery is minimal.

Although we were told James wouldn't be able to walk, at 16months old, James just got up and walked! However, due to his poor vision and his Epilepsy it is unsafe for James to walk freely. He has a Deprivation Of Liberty Safeguards in place (DOLS), whereby he can only freely walk in soft areas, these areas include his school rebound room, Rainbows soft play room and his bedroom at home which was created purposely for him to be able to walk around and sleep in safely without the risk of injury. We raised the funds for this room via local charities and it's a game changer; he has so much freedom in there. This all came about because in just over a year's period, he had 22 A&E admissions due to falls and seizures that resulted in injury. Some of those injuries were so severe that he repeatedly hit his head, broke his nose and split open his eyebrow (which required gluing back together). His chin was constantly taking the full force of the drop and it is now badly scarred from stitching and gluing back together and he has also needed stitches in his lip and he has lost teeth due to impact. So, you can see that walking is a dangerous task for James.

He also has hypermobility, which makes walking a challenge, as he is super flexible; so, he now wears splints, which has helped him greatly. James is a wheelchair user and needs at least a 2:1 ratio for transferring. He relies on adults for all his care needs to be met; he needs help feeding and because he is a high choking risk, his food needs to be soft and cut up very small. James is non-verbal, Severely Visually Impaired, uses a walker to help him safely move about in unpadded large open spaces and he wears a helmet. James doesn't sleep well at night and often has seizures during this time. This means he cannot be left alone when awake in case he has a seizure during the night which means I get very little sleep too. James also requires many different medications to routinely be given throughout the day. I am James's full-time carer, his advocate, his taxi, pharmacist, his nurse, his entertainer, cook and cleaner. I meet all his basic care needs- including hygiene and pad changes.

We have added a little sister for James into the mix in 2021, and they love each other. James has taught her how to blow raspberries and she has shown him love and kindness. The bond they have together is special. Seeing Emily cuddling up to James is beautiful and at the age of 3, she is able to shout for help when he is having a seizure, or if he's fallen down and hurt himself.

A charity that I was put in touch with to support our family was Home-Start. I was really struggling at this point, hardly able to think straight and I had given up work to care for James. James was on the Ketogenic diet, which required specific and hard to find foods - it took time and energy to prepare. With James unable to be left alone, I had no time at all. So, my volunteer would take James swimming, to baby groups, and help me with James's care whilst I completed simple tasks. She was excellent. I would not have got through those early years without her support. Just to have someone to speak to makes all the difference in the world. She understood exactly what I was going through, she listened and she impacted mine and James' lives massively. Also, after I gave birth to Emily, things were really bad at home with James. He was always in and out of hospital, and with Ashley working and having a new born baby, I was struggling. So, Emily's Health Visitor (the same one that James had!) got me back in touch with

Home-start and I was able to have the support from the same Home-start volunteer, the lady who helped me with James, how amazing! It was a real blessing that at the time I needed the help and support, this wonderful lady was free and able to offer us support again.

After our local nursery couldn't meet James' needs, we were told about a specialist setting. Well, I am so, so glad that she made me aware of this wonderful place because as soon as I walked through the doors and met their lovely head teacher, I knew that this was the right place for James and the right environment for him to have all his needs met. Why had I been so worried? I think that the honest answer to that question, is that it was my last glimmer of hope that James would miraculously get better, be cured and be able to attend a mainstream setting without any problems, like all of his friends. I believed that I was giving up by sending him to a nursery that I had never heard of before and which was miles away from our home. It was here that I realised that we were on a different path than I had originally envisioned. I had to give myself a little shake; it wasn't about me and what I wanted anymore. It was about James, what he needed and what was right for him. It was here that a switch went off in my head and I understood that James would need a lot more support than I had originally realised. I would need to stand up for him and make some hard choices that I may not like, but were vital to James and his education and wellbeing.

At this wonderful setting, James developed in so many ways, he made us proud every day. We had amazing days, and stressful ones too. I was constantly on edge every time my phone rang. I was worried it was because James was ill, (he often had 999 callouts due to seizures, non-breathing episodes, which left him blue and bumps to the head due to his seizures.) The team that worked with James were absolutely amazing and always had his best interests at heart going above and beyond in all aspects of his care. On one occasion, James had a blue episode and the ambulance couldn't wait for me to arrive, so staff went in the ambulance so James wasn't alone!

It was during this time that I was introduced and referred to Zoe's Place, a baby hospice in Coventry that looks after poorly babies and offers respite to their families. Having the break for a few hours each month was really important for us; we were exhausted as a family and going through so much that it was mentally and emotionally exhausting.

We were also introduced to the Bamboozle Theatre Company. James benefits greatly from attending performances, as their engaging and encouraging approach allows him to participate in his own way by vocalising, waving his arms, kicking his feet and by blowing raspberries! This is a massive high for us, because finding groups for James to attend are few and far between, so to be able to witness the pure joy and participation from James is an amazing opportunity. James has been attending sessions since he was 2 years old; he is almost 8 now! James loves the music, the movements and the freedom to be who he is - he comes alive! He is accepted here and he loves it; he also brings his little sister along to enjoy the fun too!

After leaving Nursery, James started school and all my fears and anxieties came back. He was about to have a massive change, during Covid, and during a period where his health was really poor and he was spending a lot of time in hospital - everything was happening all at once (doesn't it always?!). I was also pregnant with our second child during this time and I was incredibly poorly with my renal health again, and on top of that, we were in a lockdown. We found out early on that we were expecting a girl this time around, baby Emily. It was at the 16-week mark when my kidneys deteriorated again. This time we knew what to look out for and I had early intervention from the renal midwives, everything was planned perfectly (apart from Covid happening- obviously!).

When James started at school, all staff worked very closely with James; his physical health had deteriorated and he was having a lot of accidents due to falls from his poor vision and from seizures too. Another member of staff was brought in to support James, so he had two adults supporting him, who knew him well and were able to seek the right support for him. Most mornings, I would go into the school in tears due to lack of sleep from caring for James all night and from James having accidents, serious accidents, from seizures leading to falls. They were always so kind and reassuring me that it wasn't my fault, there was nothing I could have done to have prevented it and helping me to get the right support from medical professionals who might be able to help.

Eventually, after an urgent EHCP (Education Health and Care Plan) review, it was decided that James would have a DOLS put in place as he was a risk when free walking. However, in a soft and padded environment James can freely explore as much as he likes without his wheelchair, so this was implemented into his curriculum. All these positive changes were vital in keeping James safe, happy and included. The school have been involved for three years now, and they've provided us with a lot of support over the years, from getting James to do things that are out of his comfort zone to pointing us in the right direction when we have worries or concerns. We are very thankful for all they have done to support James; they have certainly made our journey a lot easier.

Another special support network that we have, comes in the form of Rainbows Hospice for Children and Young People. Over the past couple of years, we have been to Rainbows for family fun days, play days, had massages with the therapy team, family swim sessions, parent carer sessions, coffee mornings and respite stays. We have been closely connected with the hospice; they are very important to us. We have a family support worker assigned to us and we can go to her for any support or with any questions that we may have. James loves his overnight stays, he goes swimming every day, has a feast in the dining room and is able to use the soft play room, music therapy, go to their built-in cinema room, sensory room and the children's lounge where he can share stories and relax with his friends. It's an amazing place. James's face lights up as soon as we walk through their doors - it's a home-from-home environment.

Our community has helped us to grow too, our local Church are our family;

they offer emotional and practical support in times of stress and joy and everything in-between! They've supported James in so many different and personal ways which helped us to meet his needs over the past few years. They smile as James greets them all with his raspberries and it's a relief to know that they are with us on our journey, praying with us along the way. They ensure he is included in all their activities and this is very important for us.

James attends FTM Dance sessions (Forward Thinking Movement and Dance) over the summer holidays. This is vital to us as it breaks up the long summer holidays when we don't have the usual school support. FTM Dance care for James on a 1:1 basis, they engage James in sessions that allow him to be creative in his wheelchair with his friends. This respite gives James the encouragement he needs in order to creatively develop, he looks forward to attending these sessions and interacting with everyone there.

We also have Diana Nurses involved in our care; they provide his medical equipment on a monthly basis. They look after James; they know him really well - his likes and his dislikes. We treasure their support. They make challenges seem much smaller, they free up my time and they ensure I am getting the rest I need whilst Ashley is at work. They know how to care for James in a way that doesn't interfere with our home life. The ladies assigned to James come in and work their magic. Seeing the bond James has created with each staff member brings tears of love and joy to us. They are not only excellent with James, but they also include Emily in all their activities.

We really have had some challenges over the past few years, but everyone mentioned above has made things easier and more bearable. It is very scary living with the seriously dangerous health conditions that James has. Sometimes we are up day and night watching over him. It has taken a long time, with years of fighting for James. Fortunately, we now have a really good support network that assist and take over when we need them to. For that we are thankful. Without this support, we would be burnt out and unable to meet James's basic care needs.

What has James taught us? Well, he has taught us to be forgiving, patient, adapt our way of thinking and go with the flow. Honestly, everything has changed. Little things that were once important to us, are now irrelevant. We count the smiles, the laughs and the raspberries. They're what is important to us right now! The cuddles, the hand holding and the steps we make together. He has a unique way of beating the odds, of escaping the unescapable and of keeping everyone on their toes. James has introduced us to so many wonderful and caring people and our lives are totally blessed. Each person has touched our hearts in more ways than one. I used to find it difficult to ask for help, I thought I would be judged for not being able to cope or for being unable to care for my own son. But I realise now that it takes strength to ask for help, to go through the things we have gone through and survive and I am proud. Through all the stress and exhaustion, the unknown, the medical appointments that never end and the A&E trips that eat into our lives, we made it, and we continue to make it. Yes, there are tears, but there are smiles too.

I want to say a massive thank you to everyone involved in the care of James, you are all very special to us and we appreciate each and every one of you.

Oh, the things I have learnt

By Alison Hunter-Lehman

Alison, lives in Desborough, Northamptonshire. She is a Mum to three autistic children. Her husband is American and also autistic; he received his diagnosis when he was 40. Alison has always worked with children, she has been a nanny, an LSA in primary schools, and also worked in nursery schools. At 50 she completed a degree in SEN/Autism/Children and became licensed to run the National Autistic Society's Early Bird Plus programme, which is what she does now.

Oh, the things I have learnt

I have decided to tell our story, with the hope that this helps parents understand Autism and their autistic children. Autism came into my life officially in October of 2004 with the diagnosis of our middle son who was 3 years old. It has always been there in the family, however, we just didn't recognise it as Autism.

We had been living and working in India, in the foothills of the Himalayas at an international boarding school. My husband was teaching IT and running the elementary school's computer lab. When we arrived in January 2000, we had one 2 and 1/2 year-old son, and I was pregnant with our second. My son was, what I thought a little quirky, his speech wasn't delayed, as such, he had lots of language, but my husband and I seemed to be the only ones who could understand him. As the school children and staff were from all around the world, there were many different cultures all blending, so I didn't pay much attention to his quirks. My baby was due at the end of June, so in March of 2001, I flew home to the UK to prepare for his birth. My pregnancy was fine, apart from the fact I felt sick for the first 14 weeks. I did all the right things, stopped drinking caffeine, took my pre-natal vitamins, ate as healthily as I could.

My parents lived in an enormous vicarage in Surrey, England, which was great as they had plenty of room for myself and my eldest son to stay. Whilst there, I began to notice some differences in my eldest, he couldn't seem to sit still, and he talked non-stop. He also liked his food separated on the plate, nothing could touch, he requested "white one rice" as his favourite thing to eat. Towards the end of my pregnancy, I found a childminder to have him for a couple of hours a week so I could have a break. The childminder reported that she found him exhausting, and impulsive. She said he wasn't naughty or malicious, just full on and non-stop. I filed all this away putting it down to having been living in the community we had been.

My second son arrived 5 weeks early covered in meconium via an emergency c-section. He was about 7 and 1/2 lbs! I am very glad he didn't go full term as he would have been about 10lbs! His brother was 9 and ½ at full term, there is no way I could have birthed a 10 pounder! He was about 3 weeks old by the time his dad was able to join us. He was just a lovely sweet, contented little chap with a large head and fat dimpled filled cheeks. He was a good sleeper and ate quite well for the first few months.

Whilst recovering at home from surgery and birth, I remember watching a programme on the BBC about families struggling with their autistic children. Whilst watching this programme, I was thinking how hard it was for those parents in the programme and that I would do anything I could if I had an autistic child, but how thankful I was that I did not. The irony of this moment is not lost on me now, as it would turn out that my middle son would be our official introduction to Autism.

We returned to India in the middle of the monsoons; we had opted to use cloth nappies, however that didn't last long as it is impossible to get anything dried during the rainy season. As time passed, our middle son didn't really develop speech in the traditional way. He would babble, and giggle, we joked that he was speaking Tibetan as we had a lot of Tibetan students at the school and to our untrained ears that is what he sounded like. He was a very happy baby, but I kind of felt like he didn't need me to keep him happy, he seemed like an independent baby to me. I know that sounds weird, an independent baby, he needed me to feed him and change him and after that he was quite content. He weaned himself from the breast by about 5 months and preferred to sit in his bouncy seat with a bottle, than to be all cuddled in close to be fed. I felt at the time that I was doing something wrong with breastfeeding that made him reject me. I have come to believe that his sensory system was being overloaded by all of that close contact.

When he was 2 and 1/2, I found I was pregnant again. I started to make plans for our new arrival. I flew home again, this time with our middle son only, leaving my husband and eldest in India. Things seemed to be pootling along well, until one morning I woke up to a very sad sound. It was a little voice crying out the word "Nanole, Nanole". This is what my middle son called his brother. I got up and went downstairs to find my middle son lying in the foetal position at the bottom of the stairs calling for his brother. He was crying and looked very sad. After this event, any words he had been using, just seemed to disappear. His language development just stopped as did his social interaction and his eye contact diminished, he just pottered about on his own without needing any of us, myself or my parents. In hindsight I can see that this was a traumatic event for my son, which triggered a typical (for an autistic child) regression. I took him to the GP. I was worried about him and wanted to make sure he didn't have an ear infection; his ears were clear but she referred us to speech and language therapy (SLT). The SLT was a lovely lady, she was very gentle and kind, she took a real interest in us. The SLT took a very detailed history of his birth and his milestones, met or unmet, his inability to respond to his name, and the loss of words that he used. During our session, the SLT had several toys for him to play with; he zoned in on the small collection of Thomas the Tank Engine toys she had. He made himself comfortable on the floor, lying on his side and lined all the trains up in order of size. He didn't look at the SLT at all, it was as if she and I weren't there, he was in his own wee world.

As we were planning to go back to India, I asked her what would happen with my son if we were living in the UK. She advised that he would be given a hearing test to see if his hearing was impaired and if that wasn't the case, then there would be further assessments to see what else might be the issue. In hindsight, it must have been very obvious to her what the issue was, no one had used the word Autism up to this point.

Our daughter was born in January of 2004, she wasn't early, and came into this world via a planned c-section. However, we stayed in hospital a long time as she was very jaundiced and had some feeding issues. Once her feeding issues were dealt with and her blood count was better, we were allowed to go home. Once again, my husband and eldest son joined us for the winter holiday but had to go back to India before myself and the two younger ones. When I did eventually fly back to India, a friend travelled with me. This was a godsend, during our flight home, I had dozed off and when I woke up my middle son had disappeared. I started looking for him, slightly panicked. I found him upstairs in the little area that the aircraft staff used to sleep. He was sitting on the floor going through someone's bag! On the way back down to our seat, a very kind and observant fellow passenger pointed out that he had been into the toilets and pulled all the toilet roll out! It was all over the floor. I was embarrassed about what he had done and felt severely judged by the helpful passenger. This would not be the last time I felt such judgement.

Upon returning to India, I booked a hearing test. The area we lived in was quite rural, so as a white family we stood out a lot; we attracted quite a bit of attention. Often tourists would ask to take pictures with us, or to take pictures of our kids, someone would usually try their English out on us. So, when we turned up for the hearing test, we were very conspicuous. My son wouldn't sit still to have the headphones over his ears, he clambered all over me, refused to let the headphones go on his head. The doctor we were seeing asked me if he was 'mentally retarded', or did he have ADHD. I was a little taken aback by these questions (there was somewhat of a language barrier between ourselves and the doctor and also a cultural divide, using words like 'mental retardation' was completely acceptable to the doctor). I had to bite my tongue and let his words roll of my back because I desperately wanted to find out where my boy's words had gone. Eventually he was given something to make him sleep. Electrodes were then placed on his head and the test was completed, showing his hearing was fine. As it happened there was an American paediatrician working at the local hospital and he agreed to do a further assessment for us. No one had used the word Autism up until this point, even then the word was used very sparingly and only as a maybe. So, by October 2004, myself, my baby and my now 3 year old were travelling back to the UK to get assessed further. I had been able to get back in contact with the SLT who had originally seen us back in 2003. Again, hindsight and knowing how the NHS works and how long everything takes, we were extremely lucky to be seen again.

We were referred to a wonderful centre in Surrey and my son had a full multi-disciplinary assessment. At the end of this, he was diagnosed with an Autism Spectrum Disorder (ASD). I was absolutely devastated, I had to call my husband in India and deliver this news, it was a really hard thing to have to do. My son's main issues are to do with his language development. He has an expressive and receptive speech disorder. No one could tell me if he would ever speak, or if he would ever be able to learn, or go to a mainstream school. I went back to India to try and figure out what we needed to do next. After the diagnosis was given, one of the SLTs said to me, "Think of your son as not being able to speak or understand English, it is like a foreign language to him". As we were living in India and surrounded by many different languages, this made sense to me. She also said that the way to get through to him might be through pictures. This was so helpful to me, I cannot even tell you, but I will try.

Back to India and the wonderful, supportive, and caring community that we were working and living in. During the next 8 months, I read books about Autism and drew pictures for my son. I drew pictures for toilet training, I drew pictures for going to school, I drew pictures of me packing up our home to return to the UK, I drew pictures of aeroplanes, trains and the house we would move into. All of this helped, which is amazing to me as my drawing skills are rubbish, but a stick figure with brown balls coming out of its bottom into a nearly unrecognisable toilet did it for my son, when it came to learning to poo in the toilet and not his pants. Once I saw how well the picture worked with him, I felt a little less unsure of how to communicate with my lovely little boy.

We arrived in England in the summer of 2005, with no jobs, an autistic child and very little knowledge of the system here. Fortunately, one of my sisters worked in our local medical centre and was able to sign post me to some things I needed to know, but most importantly she introduced me to one other mum who also has autistic children. This was a game changer for me, because of this friendship, I was able to become a founding member of a local family support group, and I was able to connect with the right professionals who could educate me, guide me, and ultimately help me understand my child.

This is not the end of the story. By 2008, our eldest had been diagnosed with ADHD/Asperger Syndrome and in 2009 our youngest was diagnosed with ADHD and finally in 2017 she was diagnosed with High Functioning Autism (a term that I hate as it implies that she functions highly in all things). As with any autistic person, her struggles are varied, as are her strengths and abilities.

Throughout our journey the thing that stands out to me are the wonderful people I have met, other mums who just know what it is like, where you don't need to explain your situation, they just get it. I have found my tribe. I have learned so much through this journey my kids and I have been on for the past 25 years, and what I have learned will forever be engraved in my heart and soul. I have learned to accept difference; I have become a better, kinder, less judgemental person for having the children I have.

Our expectations vs reality- wouldn't change them for the world but I'd love to change the world for them

By Sam Broughton (nee Andrews)

Sam is a mum to two neurodivergent sons and a daughter. Sam also has AuDHD and Dyspraxia and many other health conditions that often co-exist with being part of the Neurodivergent community.

Each poem is a dedication to each of her children. "They have taught me so much not just about themselves and their journeys have all been so different but also that it was okay for me to embrace my difference too."

Sam became a counsellor who now works predominantly with Neurodivergent clients. She supports individuals that are part of the Neurodivergent community with so many different aspects of their lives.

Email- sam@yourelementz.com
Website- www.yourelementz.com - This is your time, to get the support you deserve!

"Whether you're a parent, sibling or child (13+) diagnosed, or on the pathway to finding out. It's okay if you don't want to know, either way, I am here to support you with whatever your journey has led you through in a way that suits your needs."

Our expectations vs reality- wouldn't change them for the world but I'd love to change the world for them

Where do I start? Get strapped in here we go....

This rollercoaster of parenthood took so many twists and turns.

Who knew where it would go?

My first born, what an adventure

Exciting and nervous all in one go.

Exciting dreams goals and plans,

Who knew what life had in store then?

Nothing went as planned!

Such a chilled out baby, but hungry all the time

I wanted to do everything the right way

Although everyone had a different plan.

Single mum now at 20, so what did I know?

Offered tranquillisers at 4 to help him sleep

No thanks 'I think this runs way more deep!'

It only helped him get to sleep.

We did take them and that helped for a while

Till they removed them 3 years later.... Now where do we go?

School was tough, always led astray by one or another,

In trouble all the time, no positive interventions offered!

Why couldn't they see the sweet, kind, polite and caring son I was raising?

I guess the chaos of school hid him from their sight?

Change his schools? Yeah I did twice

All said the right things when we came through the door,

All they saw was his behaviour, not that they were causing it.

At home all the upset of years and anger too

At the injustice of the boy who they saw

Who wasn't who he was.

Why could no one see his struggles? I fought and I fought.

Gp- 'An Autism diagnosis - are you sure you want this label?'

Shamed in that office, I'm only a parent what do I know?

Left school, no qualifications gained, the environment still not right.

A low self esteem caused and held that weight over his life.

17 came an Autism diagnosis when mental health took its toll.

18 came ADHD, when life- work, relationships and all felt too much

Then Covid hit... no meds, no support and on our own again.

My boy (now man) has so many conditions that make his life tough

Asthma, Type 1 Diabetes and a nut allergy to top it off.

His life hasn't been easy but I'm so proud of the man he's become

Next chapter, a father himself now to come.

Message for Josh- You face so much, you survived even more

Now's the time to live and carve out the future you deserve!

………………………………………………………
………….

Second born, 11 years later. By then new partner, new career.

So much like his big brother,

Quick to learn and get on his feet

Hit all the right milestones, early in fact

Then boom vaccinations, regressed just like that

No words uttered since.

Plate, fork and spoon refused after that.

Reset switch was pressed and that was that!

Always loved the water, phew he never lost that

Hopeful many said he might get other things back.

Took him to nursery for support

As I thought I was going mad

If it wasn't for his red book

Other memories and videos that proved he did that.

How could this be happening?

I just wanted to understand

Took him to the doctors

They couldn't argue with facts,

Sent straight to paediatrician.

Everything moved quick after that.

Council were notified instantly.

A nursery place followed soon after that

What an amazing service

Staff and facilities helped him so much.

Eye contact went from 0 to 50 and name recognition came back

Speech and language taught us Makaton actions and basic words

Even PECS too.

But he understands language so rejected a new thing for him to do

So many great charities, people's experiences and organisations

Offering training, support for parents

Days out and respite made accessible

His confidence soared after diagnosis was gained.

Never known such determination

Such drive to be understood

With no words, no way of communicating

Frustration ensued

So much paperwork, to get what he deserved

Why do they make things so difficult? Just to access the basics

He lights up the room

With his smile and charisma

Everyone knows his name

And wants to be around him

He has no awareness of danger

Always searching for his next adrenaline high

Scaling eight foot fences easy peasy for him

The rest of us having to encourage him down

AAC device changed him again

So much more he could share

His understanding, his knowledge and challenges now shared.

Sensory seeker by nature

His sensory diet demands a lot

Pain threshold so high you have to interpret the lot.

We've been through blood test, dental surgeries

His strength and resilience we admire in awe.

As each new adventure or trauma starts the next chapter or plot,

He takes everything in his stride.

Bounces back, so quick, it's a shock!

Our fears are just that.

Ours alone, to carry and navigate through

He'll be amazing, be himself

No matter what.

We love your personality,

Your spark and your smile

We'll always be alongside you

For as long as you need us.

Message for Logan- Never let this world change you, you are exactly who you were born to be... a beautiful individual soul, we are grateful to have you in our lives!

....

Last but not least

When our daughter arrived

She flew into this world

Boom, I'm here I've arrived

She rivalled the boys in all their milestones

Potty trained and hyperlexic

Not yet two years old

She absorbed information like a sponge

Yet slept very little

Moods either serious or laughing

There's no in between.

She organises in rainbows

No just lining up here

Enigmatic, loves people

There's no Autism here.

As her brother got support

Quite quickly only a year gap here

Such a different journey

With health visitor, GP and paediatrician

thinking- there's nothing to do here

When her brother moved on to a specialist setting

She was still in mainstream nursery

No brother just being there to keep her feeling safe.

Wait hold on, we didn't know that

Her brother was the crutch and a role model to watch.

Twinship some may call it

They even got called that.

Two opposite sides in so many ways

She needed him, but we couldn't take him back.

Two nursery placement breakdowns later and yet no help in sight.

Paediatrician only going on her academics

She's bright we never contested that.

Her sensory profile was spiky to look at

Putting on clothing and hair washing like torture

Socialising she craved, someone to play with

Yet not understanding the rules made it hard.

Intensive friendships

All in or all out

Such a social butterfly

If that's what you saw, she wore a good mask

EHCP refused, too clever for that.

Yet no help or support with social, emotional and communication struggles

And meltdowns after school everyday.

All they saw was her mask.

But she could only hold it in for so long

Some days she'd become mute.

There was also hyper days too.

Emotional regulation- still finding new ways to help her with that.

To express it safely and recover

Our girl never wants to stand out for being different . I wish she could see what we see her difference makes her shine brighter.

Message to Keira- we will always have your corner, face each challenge by your side, with you and for you, we'll be the support and the guide!

Our journey of courage

By Natalie Greenall

Natalie Greenall is a Mum and carer for her 3-year-old son who has Spinal Muscular Atrophy Type 1. This is a severe genetic condition that develops in babies less than 6 months old. It makes the muscles weaker and causes problems with movement, feeding and breathing. It's a serious condition that gets worse over time, but thankfully there are now treatments available to help manage the symptoms and to hopefully prolong life expectancy. Natalie lives with her husband and son in Warrington in the North West of England.

Our journey of courage

Our son Theo has Spinal Muscular Atrophy Type 1 (SMA) which is a severe genetic condition in babies. Before the term SMA was uttered to us, our journey of planning for a family and our pregnancy journey seemed smooth, even despite being pregnant throughout the Covid pandemic. As everything seemed fine, and no issues had arisen ,our gorgeous boy Theo was born 2 weeks after his due date.

Labour progressed quite slowly and the doctors stated the safest way to get our baby out was by emergency C-Section. This was the scariest moment of my life but also so reassuring that labour would be over soon! Within 20 minutes I was taken to Theatre and my husband was prepped and dressed in scrubs ready to join me. Very quickly we were introduced to our precious baby boy who weighed a huge 10lb 3oz. He was wrapped in a beautiful knitted blanket and his journey on this Earth had now begun.

Recovery went well and after one night on the maternity ward myself and Theo (our newest edition) were discharged from hospital. My husband was delighted to have his family together and we continued our journey in our family home.

We had regular visits from the community midwives and health visitor which included the newborn screening heel prick. This came back normal after about 3 days. During this time, we had lots of family visits and we were besotted by our blue-eyed boy! As a first-time parent it seemed like we had such a perfect recovery and most importantly a healthy baby who passed all checks in order to return home.

But, on day 10, things changed dramatically, the journey then took a downward spiral and it soon became apparent that things weren't as smooth as it seemed. The perfect family image we were living became less of a reality and very quickly over the next few days and weeks our lives plummeted to a devastating situation. We were admitted to our local children's ward due to our son being 'floppy' and 'not passing reflex checks'. Lots of tests were done and all seemed to come back normal. The last tests that doctors wanted to do were genetic bloods. We agreed to this and then returned home whilst we awaited for the results.

Around 4 days later, we got a telephone call stating we needed to pack a bag and take our baby to another hospital further afield. We presumed it could be either for further tests or maybe for the dreaded genetic results. Unfortunately for us it was the latter option, the results had returned and we had a meeting with the Neuromuscular team of around 10 doctors and professionals. I can still remember that Friday afternoon so vividly in my mind: the time, smell, the saddened eyes on the professionals who wore masks. 'Your son has Spinal Muscular Atrophy Type 1,' said the Consultant.

Although after diagnosis, a life expectancy of 18 months was given for our precious baby, we were extremely lucky to be given the chance of pioneering treatment options for our baby. He is now progressing well, meeting small milestones and has recently celebrated his 3rd Birthday! It's been a rollercoaster of a journey and we still have lots of unexpected hospital trips, but with a knowledgeable team of professionals, dedicated care workers and a loving family, we are the best team we can be for our boy Theo. He has taught us to make the most of each day, create lots of memories together and to love with everything we have!

I don't know how you do it? You are amazing!

By Tina Fox

Tina Fox is a Mum, Nurse and Carer for Daniel who is 8 years old. They live together in West Sussex.
"I chose this title because I have lost track over the years of how many people have said that to me! I don't think I am any more amazing than any other parent who would do anything for their children."

I don't know how you do it? You are amazing!

Our family started back in 2005 when myself and my husband met. Fast forward a few years, we had two daughters, Olivia and Chloe. We tried for a few years to get pregnant again and finally, after a miscarriage, in 2014, we found out we were expecting. Apart from a few aches and pains, and being classed as a geriatric mum (I was 34!), my pregnancy was uncomplicated. We didn't find out the sex of any of our children, but Jon had told me he would divorce me if we had another girl! In May 2015, ten days overdue, Daniel was born at home. It was a planned homebirth as I had also had with my girls. I had a three hour labour, which the Midwife described as a 'blue birth', purely based on my language! In all my labours my babies were all 'back-to-back', so I had loads of pain in an already painful back! My waters never went in labour, and Daniel was born in the sac which is very rare (1 in 80,000 births)! From the day he was born, he has always been unique and done things in his own time! When he was born, Olivia was 9 years old and Chloe was 7 years old.

As I am writing this nearly 9 years after Daniel was born, and lots has happened, it has been tricky trying to remember what order some things happened! Also, this has been written as I have tried to remember it and how it has flowed has meant that it might not necessarily be in order.

As the Midwives were checking Daniel immediately after he was born, they noticed that he had some breathing difficulties and advised us that he should be taken into hospital, they had also noted some meconium in the sac when they burst it. They called an ambulance and I ran around the house trying to pack enough stuff for a few days in hospital. We had a rushed 'first baby picture' before getting into the ambulance. Unfortunately, we didn't get many pictures in those first few days. When we got to the hospital, we walked up to the Special Care Baby Unit (SCBU). When in the lift I told the Paramedic that I didn't feel very well, and was told to sit on the floor. In

SCBU I felt unwell again, really dizzy; they thought I was worried about my baby being cannulated. The next few hours are a bit of a blur to me. I collapsed a few times and had a large post-partum haemorrhage. I ended up on the Delivery Suite with lots of interventions and my husband stayed with Daniel in SCBU, until they decided Daniel was stable enough and he joined me. We were discharged a couple of days later after Daniel had intravenous antibiotics and I had lots of iron!

Normal family life continued at home; the girls loved their little brother and would do anything for him, which is what we blamed for his delay! That and the fact that he was a lazy boy! It was when Daniel was around seventeen months old, our journey changed direction. At this point, Daniel was rolling around the floor, with the odd bit of commando crawling, but wasn't sitting up, was showing no interest in walking and only had one word "dadad". We noticed that Daniel used to thrash his head around, and I had concerns that he couldn't hear us. I went to the local clinic to get him weighed and asked the Health Visitor if she would be able to refer Daniel for a hearing test. I felt he had Glue ear as he had recurrent ear infections. She wanted to come and see Daniel at home, so came around the next day. She immediately referred Daniel to the Community Paediatrician, and we were seen the next day as they were concerned that Daniel had something wrong neurologically. We saw the Paediatrician and he ruled out anything neurological, but he did have concerns that Daniel was delayed. The Paediatrician sent us off for blood tests, including Chromosome bloods. My Husband didn't come with me when I went to the Paediatrician for the blood results as we both felt he was just a lazy boy. The Paediatrician told me that Daniel had a Chromosomal abnormality and he wanted us to see a Geneticist. I then had to ring my Husband at work to tell him that there actually was something wrong with our gorgeous boy. We met with the Geneticist who told us Daniel has Mosaic Ring Chromosome 8. We were told it was almost a whole extra Chromosome and was ring shaped instead of straight. At the time the only thing known about Chromosome 8 was that it affects development. We were given a leaflet with very limited information, and were referred to Physio, Speech and Language Therapy, and Portage, and met the Special Needs

Health Visitor. Around this time, we also started going to the local group for children with additional needs. It was scary how quickly our lives had changed direction and we had entered on the path of being Special Needs parents. It was whilst chatting to a staff member at this group about how little support there was for us, frustrated that not enough was being done for our son, that they mentioned a local charity who might be able to help.

That charity was the best thing that happened to us. We started at The Dame Vera Lynn Children's Charity on Daniel's second birthday. He was still not sitting up and had no speech. Daniel started weekly conductive education sessions with them; it was also a fantastic opportunity to meet other special needs families. The charity were so supportive, they also provided swimming lessons for Daniel in a heated pool with specialist swimming instructors and even a Speech and Language therapist. All the staff there gave us information and the knowledge we needed to help Daniel. The Speech and Language Therapist taught me how to use PECS to support Daniel. I even paid for a Makaton course as I didn't want Daniel to never be able to communicate. I really didn't want an angry child who was not able to tell us what he needed to. At the same time, Daniel was still having physio sessions with the NHS. He really didn't engage with these; he much preferred the Conductive Education which was more fun for him. In his regular physio sessions, Daniel would quite often close his eyes and refuse to do anything! The conductive education changed this behaviour, once he realised it was more fun! They also did lots of messy play with the children. Daniel hated this so much! He wouldn't even touch the grass! He hated all forms of messy play, paint or any different textures, even the spiky balls they used in the sessions. The best photo we have of Daniel is him sat on a sandy beach, completely covered in sand and even eating it, but that took about a year of messy play sessions to get to that! Even now he can sometimes be wary of touching some things, but he now loves getting messy and one of his favourite things is to be outside in forest school.

Eventually Daniel did get a hearing test which proved that he had barely any hearing due to Glue ear, and was referred to ENT, it would appear that I did know my child! They decided to fit him with grommets. The day of the surgery I took Daniel down to the anaesthetic room as only one parent is ever allowed. It was tough as he really didn't understand what was happening. One of the team tried talking to Daniel to explain what was happening as they didn't understand his needs. I had to be 'that parent' and explain there was no point in telling Daniel, no bubbles or other distraction techniques would work as it would just be longer for him to get worked up. All went well with the surgery, and life continued as before. Not long after at one of his appointments for a hearing test, it was found that one of the grommets had fallen out and the other wasn't doing what it should. They mentioned that they would usually then try hearing aids but there was no point as Daniel wouldn't understand and wouldn't keep them in. I argued that one, I explained that they at least needed to give him a chance to be able to keep them in and have a chance at being able to hear. He was already so behind the other kids his age, and not being able to hear would put him even further behind. They did agree and so he was measured up for hearing aids. We went back to have them fitted and he tried to take them out once whilst we were there and he never took them out again in all the time that he had them. The difference in him after that was amazing. His speech massively improved, and he started to have some understanding. Covid also helped develop his communication skills. The joys of having two parents who were working for the NHS meant Daniel was one of the few who got to go to school, and with much smaller than normal class numbers he showed huge improvement. He hasn't had his hearing aids for about two years now as he seems to have grown out of the glue ear. He does still have to have yearly hearing tests to monitor this.

Early on I spoke to the Speech and Language therapist about Daniel's eating. I had concerns that he didn't chew food properly and would keep taking food in and out of his mouth. It took me six months of keep telling them until they finally gave in and came round to our house to watch Daniel eat. Oh, and funnily enough I was right, he can't chew properly. She explained that he wasn't using his tongue to move the food to the back of his mouth and that was what he was doing when he took the food out and put it back in. We were given different things to try but nothing ever helped. He even had a couple of choking episodes whilst he was at playgroup, so for years he had to have a 1 to 1 for every meal to make sure he didn't choke. That has only been stopped in the last year at school because we now send him in with lunch and we only give him 'safe' foods. I did speak to the Speech and Language therapist at the charity and asked her and she felt that Daniel had a tongue tie which had never been picked up, but she said at his age they will only operate if it affects his speech, which even now we can't prove as he still has delayed speech.

At one of our earlier appointments, I raised my concerns with the Paediatrician about Daniel's vomiting. It wasn't every day so he wasn't concerned. After about a year I did ask the GP for a referral, he was even vomiting silently in his sleep. We kept a food diary but there was nothing obvious that was causing it. The GP referred us to our local hospital where we were seen by a Gastroenterologist. Daniel had an Endoscopy and they placed an NG tube which was to be left in to monitor the pH's and check for reflux. Due to Daniel's sensory issues, the NG tube lasted about 20 minutes after he came round from the anaesthetic! When we saw the Consultant for the results, he told us that Daniel's vomiting was behavioural. We raised our concerns about how he couldn't be deliberately vomiting whilst he was asleep. We were told there was nothing more they could do for it, so we were discharged. A while after we were staying at my sister's house, she isn't local to us so we don't see her very often. Daniel was standing in front of her TV. I noticed a look on him and knew he was about to vomit, I grabbed a bowl, caught the vomit and Daniel carried on with what he was doing. My sister pointed out that this was not normal behaviour. So, after having a conversation with a doctor at work, I requested a referral from the GP to a different Gastroenterologist. We were referred to a very large hospital, they did blood tests and did another Endoscopy. Whilst doing this Endoscopy they placed a Bravo capsule to monitor his pH's. Nothing for Daniel to pull out really helped, all he had was a box he had to wear for a week. We went back for the results and they told us Daniel didn't have Reflux and we were told the only option was surgery to tighten the top of his stomach. We said no to this as he would still feel sick and would retch but not be able to be sick. We felt this wouldn't be fair on a child with no understanding, so continued with putting up with the vomiting episodes. Daniel didn't have the understanding or the communication to be able to tell us when he was going to be sick so we would always be changing him and cleaning up vomit. We asked the GP to refer us back to see if there was anything else that the Gastro team could offer. As this was throughout the Covid Pandemic, we had a telephone call appointment with the Doctor. He said that the results from the previous Bravo capsule had been read wrong and Daniel did in fact have Reflux. It was so frustrating, that this had been missed. Daniel was started on medication which has improved his symptoms but we still have a fair bit of vomit so we are currently undergoing more tests and waiting for yet more results. Because of all the vomiting, Daniel ended up having 12 teeth removed. I took him to the Special Dentistry service as Daniel was always reluctant to lay on the chair or let them look in his mouth. The Dentist managed to have a look in his mouth and told me that he had multiple cavities where the teeth had been eroded from all the vomit. I cried that day too, the poor Dentist! I felt like such an awful mum, having not noticed that his teeth were that bad. We had been regularly taking him to a Dentist, who had all along said that from what they could see everything looked fine. Daniel was amazing with the surgery, he was eating crisps within about 20 minutes of waking up, and he didn't let the lack of teeth stop him eating! We had a consultation with the Dietician about a pureed diet ready to make sure he was still eating but it was never needed!

Over the years Daniel has added to his list of diagnoses, I can't remember exactly when he got them all! Mosaic Ring Chromosome 8, Global Developmental Delay, Glue ear, Hypermobility (he has very poor core stability), sensory processing disorder and his most recent was his Autism diagnosis. I have no doubts that Daniel is Autistic but it amuses me that they did all the tests before his hearing aids, and then based most of the diagnosis on his lack of communication skills! Then his Paediatrician went off sick and we were given the diagnosis by another Paediatrician who had never even met Daniel! We didn't know much about Sensory Processing

Disorder and how to support Daniel best with this, so my Parents paid for Daniel to have a full assessment with a local private Occupational Therapist. They provided us with a huge breakdown of Daniel's behaviours and gave us a sensory diet of ideas of what Daniel responded best to. We had found it quite difficult to calm him down sometimes and they suggested in their report that Daniel responded well to vibrations and spinning, so we brought him a vibrating cushion which we would hold against him to calm him. The worst sensory issues he had were haircuts, nail cutting and teeth cleaning. We have tried everything over the years! The only thing that has worked is perseverance! We have tried bribery, pinning him, technology, nothing has ever really worked with him. I even injured my wrist trying to hold Daniel to cut his finger nails and now I am waiting for surgery. The teeth have been a big expense! I think we have tried every toothpaste and every toothbrush that has ever existed! We have finally settled with a denture brush, which is silicone rather than bristles, at least he will actually put that willingly in his mouth, he still really just chews the brush but it is all progress.

We have also had a blue badge for a few years now and it makes our lives so much easier. Being able to fully open the car door really helps when Daniel is tired and struggling to climb into the car and the risk of him running off as he has no danger awareness. There have been a couple of times that people have confronted us for parking in a disabled space. One in particular has stuck with me. Daniel was around 4 years old, and didn't have any visible disabilities. He had just finished playgroup, which was only a short distance from the disabled parking, so I hadn't taken the buggy, I made him walk. A woman actually shouted abuse at me for parking in a disabled bay, even when I showed her the blue badge, she said that we clearly didn't need it.

The school process was very stressful. We had the paediatrician suggesting that we look at the local Special Needs school, and his physio was telling us that Daniel should not go to the local Special Needs school as he would never be motivated to walk, as no one there walks. We were still in the process of applying for his EHCP which we would need for him to get into the SEN school. We did go and look at the SEN school; myself and my husband had a tour with some other parents. It is tough looking around a school like that trying to imagine where your child is going to fit in, but we could see the huge benefits of getting him in there. We were told that there were only 8 places in Reception and there was always lots of people wanting places. For that reason, we were advised to look around the local mainstream schools in case we didn't get a space. We had already ruled out the Primary school that the girls had gone to as we knew it wouldn't be the right place for Daniel. The first open morning I went to was at a school with a speech unit attached to it, it had sounded ideal for Daniel. I was on my own for this one (the joys of shift work), we were given a talk by the Headteacher and I hated every minute of it, listening to her talking about what would be expected of the children, knowing that Daniel wouldn't fit into their routines. At the end of the tour, I asked if I could talk to the SENCO and that was even more traumatic. We discussed Daniel's needs and where he was developmentally and in a very roundabout way the SENCO told me that the school was not for Daniel as they wouldn't cope with him. I cried after that visit; I was so stressed wondering if we would find somewhere he could thrive. I dreaded the rest of the school tours, but I did them all with an open mind. There was one school myself and my husband had already decided we didn't want him to go to. Again, I was on my own for that open morning, I was advised to chat with the Headteacher after the tour which I did. I was very pleasantly surprised. She had said it wouldn't be ideal for Daniel if he didn't get the SEN school, but if we got him into their school then they would do everything they could to support him with everything he needed. I managed to convince my Husband to go back for a second visit with Daniel and more of a discussion and they were fantastic, so this was the school we put as our first choice of mainstream! Luckily for us, and Daniel, we got a place for him at the local SEN school, we were told after that there were over 30 children for the 8 places. We had really doubted whether he would get a place as we had felt that he wasn't disabled enough! The whole EHCP process was long, and we had it far easier than some of the stories I have heard! We were lucky that Daniel was at a fantastic playgroup who had a few disabled children and were amazing at supporting us through the whole process.

Daniel was in a cot still until the age of about 5 years old; he never tried to climb out so we left him in it. When we put him in a bed, he went into his sister's old bed which had sides, so was ideal for him. It wasn't until we went on our first holiday without the travel cot that we realised we had a problem with his sleeping. The first night of our holiday, not long after Daniel had fallen asleep, he fell out of bed, and it took us ages to calm him down. He wouldn't get back in the bed, he was so upset. We ended up having to put the mattress on the floor with pillows around it and that is what we have done every holiday since. He fidgets so much in his sleep he would fall out of bed again.

In 2020, during the warm summer I happened to notice that Daniel had a curvature to his spine, which I mentioned to his physio and she referred him to be seen. We were seen by the Consultant who agreed he had a curvature, but it was not anything we needed to be concerned about now. She did say that because we didn't know much about his chromosomal abnormality that his spine may get worse over the years, but she was happy for us to monitor it and get referred back if we had further concerns.

We were recently referred to the continence team as Daniel is still in nappies. We were referred in 2020 but nothing happened due to covid. Over the years we have tried every nappy and pull up going! It was difficult when he grew out of children's sizes as I was then guessing on sizes and ordering different products off the internet to try. Daniel had a huge issue with being naked. I'm not sure why, it just gradually got worse over the years. None of the professionals we saw knew how best to deal with it. If you took his nappy off, he would cross his legs, and even try and walk with his legs crossed. Changing his nappy in public was really hard work, sometimes we would even limit the amount of drink he had just so we didn't have to change his nappy. We tried books, we tried having weighted toys on his lap, distraction toys, a boy doll for him to take everywhere which we left naked. It even made bathing him hard work as he hated being naked. The Paediatrician had suggested bathing him with swimming trunks on but I just felt that was just creating another problem. Again though, perseverance paid off, and a few months ago Daniel got out of the bath and didn't cross his legs! Not long after that he refused to lie on the floor for nappy changes. That took a bit of getting used to, changing a nappy against gravity, but it is another small sign of progress. We are now having regular appointments with the continence team; they have loads of ideas about what we should be doing but they don't know Daniel and don't seem to listen to what we are saying works for him and us but we have to keep going with it because at least we finally get free nappies!

Because of Daniel, we have had some amazing experiences, we have done some charity work and sponsored events. I did a skydive and myself and my husband did an abseil down the side of a castle! We did all this to raise money for the fantastic charity which had done so much to help us. Our youngest daughter is now looking forward to doing her work experience at Daniel's school. Our girls have experienced so much, having a brother with additional needs, and it has made them so much more understanding of other people's needs.

A couple of years ago I was approached by the local University to speak to some of their students who were going into Nursing about our experiences. I had some fantastic feedback from the first session and it has become a regular session for the new students over the last couple of years. I talk to them as a Mum with a child with both physical and learning needs and they get the truth of what it is really like. I do also bring some of my work experiences into the presentation as they are relevant. I like to explain to the students that Special Needs parents spend so much time fighting (because there is always something you have to fight for), that we will quite often go into a situation ready to fight because that is what we expect. It sometimes feels like healthcare professionals don't listen, and we know our kids the best!

I have recently noticed more how disjointed NHS care is; none of the professionals have anything to do with each other and all focus on their own area. We have had the continence team telling us to give Daniel whatever he wants to drink, whilst we have the Dentist telling us that he should only have water. One professional will want us using certain equipment and another will tell us they don't want us using it or they want something else. We have a separate home OT and school OT who don't have any contact with each other. I have also noticed how so many of the professionals will tell you what you should be doing. If we were doing everything each of them wanted us to do with Daniel, I would never have time to go to work, I don't even think we would have time to sleep! It feels really intrusive when someone is coming into your home. I understand they have a job to do, but it also feels like they are criticizing everything we do, or how we have our layout in our house or the furniture we have. I have joined the additional needs group in the hospital where I work. I would really like to make changes and make it easier for those with additional needs and their parents or carers, and I have already got the hospital to recognise the Sunflower Lanyard scheme. I really like the idea of the Sunflower Lanyard. I find that people look at Daniel and can't work out his behaviour. He looks like a 'normal' 8-year-old, but he doesn't behave like one, and certainly won't respond like one. People who don't know him and talk to him are quite often put out when they speak to him and he doesn't respond to them in the way that is expected. Even the difference since we have had his wheelchair is noticeable. We only got the wheelchair a few months ago, before that we were using a buggy as Daniel gets tired and sometimes can partially dislocate his ankles. With the wheelchair, people are far more understanding and will move out of the way and expect far less from Daniel than when he was the very large 8-year-old in a buggy who just looks to them like a lazy child!

People don't understand all the "life admin" that comes with having a child with additional needs. Chasing appointments, the form filling, especially the joyous DLA forms! I have recently done those with very little time to complete them, it was a very tough few days! It is tough sometimes being a parent to a child with additional needs, but equally sometimes he is easier than the other two! Everyone's experience is individual and no one will ever understand totally what it is like. I have made some amazing friends over the years and between us our kids have a variety of additional needs, and we support each other through so much, I couldn't do this without them!

Gorgeous George

By Aimee Meggitt

Aimee Meggitt is a former SEND support coordinator; now she is a full-time carer for her 6-year-old son George who has a rare Genetic Syndrome, CTNNB1 syndrome and Epilepsy. CTNNB1 syndrome is a gene mutation. The CTNNB1 gene provides instructions for making a protein called beta-catenin. This protein is present in many types of cells and tissues, where it is primarily found at junctions that connect neighbouring cells (adherens junctions). Beta-catenin plays an important role in sticking cells together (cell adhesion) and in communication between cells. Aimee lives with George's father Jordan and George's little brother Harry, in Hull, UK.

Gorgeous George

My pregnancy was perfect, no morning sickness, not much weight gain and absolutely glowing. At just 21, I was engaged and pregnant with my first baby so excited for a little mini me. Due date approaching, I was eager to meet my perfect baby boy, however my journey to motherhood wasn't as I had read in the baby books.

George's due date came and went, and eventually I was induced on a hormone drip, 17 days past his due date. George's birth was the most exciting but the scariest day of my life. We got to 7cm dilated and the midwife said to me "Let's do some checks now Aimee, we're nearly there". She checked and I saw her face drop, "Just move onto your right side", she said again. Her face looked more and more concerned. I could just sense it. I think this is when my protective mum brain first triggered to read a professional's face knowing exactly how scared they were.

"I'm struggling to find his heart trace," she said to me. I looked over to my partner Jordan and my mum, who both looked terrified. "I'm just gonna pop some clips on his head to check more in-depth she said." The next words I hear, "No no there's nothing!" My heart dropped and right there and then everything felt like a movie.

She smashed the big red emergency button so hard with her hand and the door flung open and about 30 doctors shot in trying to tell me all different things. Their mouths were moving but there was no sound. "Aimee they are taking you to theatre," my Mum said. "Do you understand?" My mouth couldn't move, my body was in shock and I froze.

I thought my perfect little baby had gone before I even had the chance to say hello. It felt like the fastest rollercoaster of my life. Eventually, I was in theatre and George was born via emergency c-section. But this was just the start of the scary journey we were about to face.

12 hours later, George was feeding and he turned blue and couldn't catch his breath. Jordan (George's daddy) rushed him out to a midwife and luckily a consultant was on the ward and he managed to clear his airways and get him stable again. Jordan literally saved his life. They whipped him off to NICU and we were left waiting and waiting. I couldn't believe I had nearly lost my baby twice in not even 24 hours.

Once on NICU, we were told George was the poorliest baby on the unit, I looked around and I wondered how this could be. There were tiny premature babies laid in cots next to him. George was put into an induced coma and myself and his daddy sat by his cot side for 2 whole weeks. George made progress and he was allowed home, but the nightmare wasn't over. Jordan was the most amazing support throughout NICU, I knew he was terrified but he supported me. I was also kept in hospital due to high blood pressure. I felt like a zombie, just like in the c-section, people spoke to me but it was silent - there was no sound. Looking back, it feels like a dream.

George was a dream baby, happy content and smiley all the time. However around 6 months old I noticed George had a squint to his eyes and he wasn't hitting milestones as he should. I was passed off for a while as a 'first time mum' and everything would be 'alright.' But they were wrong and I was right. I went to my own doctor and he said my concerns were right and he referred us to the eye hospital and a paediatric consultant neurologist.

The eye doctor confirmed his squint and explained that he would need surgery and the neurologist ran an MRI and genetic testing. We are grateful for the most amazing professionals involved in George's life and care. The squint surgery was a success and his genetic testing came back 2 years later with a rare genetic syndrome called CTNNB1 syndrome. This is a neurodevelopment disorder and it affects all of George's life. George is now 6 and he cannot do anything independently; he cannot walk or talk. George probably never will but this is something I've accepted now, which is hard but I always tell myself, "Hope for the best, but expect the worst". This way you save your own heart.

George started the most amazing specialist school in Hull after Covid, when he was 3 years old and what a blessing that was. I was so scared to hand my vulnerable baby over to a group of strangers but on the first visit to the school I fell in love. When I first met George's teacher, I just clicked with her straight away, she could see the tension and the worry and that was because she was also a special needs mum herself and her daughter had a disability. She said to me "I was you 20 something years ago Aimee and I get it. George is in safe hands and we will look after him as if he is our own". Right there and then she became one of my favourite people in the world. He still has her now as his teacher and he adores her. She is fantastic, worth her weight in gold. She helps us out with anything we need and is never far away to give the best advice and support. Without her I don't know where we would be in this journey. She knows who she is and I want to say a huge 'Thank You' for being the kindest person in the whole world.

My advice to anyone parenting a disabled child is find your person, find the support…you will have to fight, but your child makes it all worth it. Always fight and never ever accept the word no. Their smile means you are right and you are doing good; a smile on George's face gives me so much comfort because he can't tell me he is okay but I know that he is.

George's eyes and smile will speak more than any words coming out his mouth ever could. This is not the journey I had planned or expected but it's a journey that I wouldn't change for the world.

George is the most beautiful and loving soul; he's taught me so much and most importantly he's taught me patience and what matters in the world and what doesn't.

I count my blessings twice when I count George.

Written by a very proud mum,
Aimee Meggitt

Be Careful What You Don't Wish For

By Rosie Naqvi - Dufty

Rosie is a Mum of three children aged 13,16 & 19, homemaker and full-time carer to Anila (16) who has a diagnosis of severe learning difficulties and Autism. Rosie lives with her husband and children in Surrey, England.

Be Careful What You Don't Wish For

Nobody sets out to have a disabled child, and as a speech and language therapist I had extra information to back up the prerequisite not to have a disabled child, particularly not one with Autism. It wasn't that I felt there was anything 'wrong' with having a disabled child, but I had witnessed the position that families and individuals with disabilities are automatically put into by society, which starts with 'the fight' (for resources) and probably ends with 'the fight' too. What was my problem with Autism? After all, it was the study of Autism that led me to become a speech and language therapist. I bumped into the subject by chance as an undergraduate studying linguistics, found it fascinating and consequently worked with children with Autism. Well, I did not hold out much hope for my future parent self-coping with a child that could not communicate in a 'neuro-typical' manner.

In retrospect it was understandable to want to stay as far away from 'the fight' as possible (the easy life is often the preferred life). However, I underestimated my future self and was ignorant to the powers of unconditional parent-child love and clearly had a very ableist approach to existence.

The pregnancy with Anila was straightforward; the usual exhausting experience particularly as I also had a two-year-old to entertain. A magical homebirth while everyone around me panicked (the midwife did not arrive on time), my mother - a trained midwife - although rusty, stepped in and remained a major fan of Anila from that day on. A healthy 7lb 4oz baby. At three months, Anila wasn't quite the feisty, ambitious mover and shaker of her elder sister. When on her belly, her head was barely leaving the ground. She was very observant with beautiful big blue eyes; her granny said she was like an owl, watching everything. At six months, her motor development remained slow, she was delayed, but she smiled, enjoyed a hug, and made noises. She actively kicked in her bouncer chair, maybe in a slightly repetitive way? Her uncle noticed it too, and thought it was quite funny. I noticed him noticing. I found myself becoming increasingly hyper-vigilant to other people's responses to her, nothing was officially wrong yet, but my intuition and a sense of dread was telling me to prepare for the unknown.

Anila's diagnosis of Global Developmental Delay came at 1 years old. It landed on us from a dynamic, high-achieving consultant paediatrician who was quick to articulate 'she may never walk, may have a syndrome – we will do blood tests.' I remember lots of measuring of her head with a tape measure, which seemed to me a very elementary way of working out what this little person may turn into. The nurse made cups of tea and gave us sympathetic looks, whilst hurriedly handing biscuits to our 3 and a half year old. And then we went home, shut the door watched nightly episodes of 'Band of Brothers' (World War 2 series) whilst ricocheting between emotions.

When Anila was 3 years old, it was confirmed that she did indeed have Autism. My experience of receiving the Autism diagnosis was so contrary to receiving the Global Developmental Delay diagnosis only two years previously. My husband went to work, I took along our mother's help (a lovely west-end performer who was perfect with children that love a song), I drove us home feeling quite at peace with what I already knew, while the mothers help commented she 'hadn't really noticed that Anila doesn't really do any imaginary play!'

By the time Anila turned 3, we had a house with a 5-year-old and a 6-month old. It was busy, full of life/noise. Anila loved reflections, banging pots and pans, trips to the park, swimming, ball parks, listening to good singing, Julia Donaldson stories, sensory play alongside her big sister, and watching Walt Disney movies. She did it all very differently and on her own terms, but she was undeniably incredibly cute and very engaged in life. As one would expect with a diagnosis of Autism, changes of routine, different people and noisy environments plus general frustrations caused her regular outbursts, alongside all the usual pains of toddlerhood. At 3 years 6 months, Anila was non-verbal, unable to point, walking (with an awkward gait), incontinent, needed help with all aspects of daily living. Now at 16, Anila is more confident in herself, uses picture exchange and body language very well to communicate needs, but at first glance is little different from that 3 1/2 year old of yesteryear.

These eventful early years of Anila's life of course brought shadows, but people did slowly emerge who helped us tremendously. My mother was a complete rock; she knew how to enjoy Anila and saw Anila as a whole person, not the altered/damaged human that sadly many others struggle to acclimatise too. Also, a brilliant Special Educational Needs co-ordinator who welcomed Anila into a busy London nursery (attached to a mainstream school). From Anila's 1st birthday to her 3rd, we were lucky to employ a gifted performer two afternoons a week as a 'mother's help,' she bought life and great pragmatism/acceptance to our household. We all loved her and we remain good friends to this day. Key friends and family members jumped on board and showed interest and support.

The local NHS did offer some good occupational therapy sessions, but we needed more support, so I contacted a charity called Brainwave. They provided an excellent assessment, then a home therapy programme which gave us all 'something to do' to help Anila. A sense of purpose was planted; our eldest daughter looks back fondly on the activity sessions we used to take part in to encourage Anila's development.

As so many before us, we chose to take on a legal battle with the local education authority to ensure Anila was able to attend a school she could settle into successfully. The charity 'SOS – SEN' were brilliant - they galvanised support, introducing us to professional contacts who would write independent reports, guided us on communications with the local authority, then acted as advocates and sat alongside us on the day of tribunal. They did all this for free.

The past 16 years with Anila have bought many highs, too many to list, but I will highlight the brightest moments. Her first steps held extra meaning (remember, we were told not to expect walking.) With Anila's rewarding smile, contagious high energy, and continued love of a show tune, it is often fun to be with Anila - quite liberating and of course the happy family holidays we have been able to include Anila within. Watching Anila's relationships with her sibling's ebb and flow over the years, witnessing this incredible bond with her granny. Even while granny deteriorated with dementia, the bond survived. They were great for each other. People that work with Anila really enjoy working with her, which is a big tick when you have a child that will be dependent on people for the rest of her life. Less so now the family is older, but there was a big sense of satisfaction which came from achieving 'outings' as a family. Typical activities, such as swimming or going for a walk in the woods, even soft play, would leave us feeling quite joyous that we had all left the house together and had a good time. Very little was taken for granted.

When reflecting on the challenges of raising Anila, overall, the hardest part has been the context with which we are within. Having and keeping our severely disabled child at home from birth, is a relatively new phenomena, the concept that disability is nothing other than a burden has only been slowly challenged since the 1930's. It follows then that the general population's exposure and understanding of people with severe disabilities (although improved) is limited, so people around us, neighbours, friends, and family find it difficult to know, what to say or do. We are moving in unchartered waters, and it can be very isolating. Without doubt, this links into the lack of resources and provision for Anila, for example, the closing of swimming sessions for people with disabilities during covid (understandable) …although, since covid, the unannounced move to not re-open those swimming sessions has been very sad. Presently, the general awareness of human rights around disabilities is quite low on most people's agenda. On a more specific note, leaving the house as a family has become more difficult with time; children grow, interests change. As a parent going to the cinema with my children or attending a family gathering, or just taking a break away from home, I often feel like something, or someone is missing. I have had to become accustomed to feeling dis-jointed.

Finally, what have I learnt from having Anila in my life? To really enjoy the ordinary so it becomes extraordinary, to sit in psychological discomfort and deal with it. The power of rest (unfortunately, this is not an area that is given much attention to when looking after carers). Prior to Anila, I had a set of self-limiting beliefs which included a more limited worldview. I have been fortunate to be relatively well educated and, in some ways, I may have known what the right things are to do and say for people that need support with communication, but I don't think I really appreciated their position fully. I have discovered emotional resources within myself and our marriage that 17 years ago, I could not have imagined were even a possibility. Like all parents, we are on a learning curve with our children, but Anila has no obvious 'map'. It takes great tenacity to stay focused on her pathway and it is a tremendous responsibility. I feel a mixture of vulnerability as a parent of a special needs child but also towers of strength; the two emotions collide regularly. As trite as it may sound, I now completely understand the hidden power and value in kindness.

Embracing a future we never expected

By Judith Corry

Judith Corry is a Mum, retired medical secretary and carer for her 15-year-old son, Sean, who has Periventricular Leukomalacia. (Periventricular Leukomalacia (PVL) is a type of brain injury that is most common in babies born too soon (premature) or at low birthweight. The white matter (leuko) surrounding the ventricles of the brain (periventricular) is deprived of blood and oxygen leading to softening (malacia). Periventricular Leukomalacia symptoms can range from mild to life-limiting. Most often, PVL leads to tight (spastic) muscles. PVL also increases the risk of Cerebral Palsy, Learning Disabilities and other problems with development).

Sean also has Quadriplegic Cerebral Palsy, West Syndrome Epilepsy (West syndrome is a constellation of symptoms characterised by epileptic/infantile spasms, abnormal brain wave patterns called hypsarrhythmia and intellectual disability), Cortical Blindness and PMLD (Profound and multiple learning disability).

Judith lives with her husband and two sons in Leicestershire, England.

Embracing a future we never expected

We live in Leicestershire - myself, my husband and our two sons, Liam who is 20 and Sean who is 15. Both were born prematurely and have been diagnosed with Cerebral Palsy, Liam with Left Hemiplegia and Sean with Quadriplegia. Liam's Cerebral Palsy is very mild and you would not know it now if you were to meet him but his early years were more affected. Sean has Bilateral Leukomalacia which can happen when a baby is born before 32 weeks and he was born at 31 weeks. This caused the Cerebral Palsy which affects his whole body, Epilepsy and Cortical Blindness.

Growing up I suffered with back pain but the reason for this was not investigated until I was twenty, when I had left home. I went for X-rays and scans which revealed that I have a prolapsed vertebrae (spondylolisthesis - level 5 slippage of vertebrae). Because of this, my orthopaedic consultant explained to me that if I ever had children that I would not be able to give birth naturally as there was the risk of the baby getting stuck in the birth canal. So, from that time on I always knew that I would need to have a Caesarean.

Many years later when I was married and became pregnant with Liam, I mentioned this when attending the antenatal clinic at the hospital but felt I was not listened to and that they did not understand. My midwife at my doctor's surgery contacted my orthopaedic consultant and my back condition and the risks around natural childbirth for me were confirmed and explained in a letter. From this point on I was taken more seriously and was booked in for a Caesarean before my due date.

I struggled a lot with the pregnancy as I grew in size, as this put extra pressure on my back. I went to see a physiotherapist who provided me with a waist support to help support my back and baby bump. It was the hottest summer since the 70's in 2003 and as time went on, I suffered with swollen and painful ankles. I also had high blood pressure and had protein in my urine. I was closely monitored and I was admitted to hospital at 34 weeks for bed rest.

After a couple of days in hospital, I was allowed home on the understanding that I would probably be back soon. I didn't realise how right they were until two days later when my waters broke. When I arrived at hospital and was examined by the obstetrician, I explained that I was booked in for a Caesarean because of my back condition. They said that because the baby was going to be 5 1/2 weeks premature, he would be a small baby and that I would be able to give birth naturally. They got me to push but unfortunately, he did get stuck in the birth canal. They could feel his head but he got stuck and so they had to rush me to theatre to do an emergency Caesarean which was made hard because they had to pull him back and out. It felt like I was being really tugged about trying to get him out and when Liam was born, he was very bruised and they thought his arm may have been broken. He was taken away to the neonatal unit straight away and I didn't even get a glimpse of him which I found heartbreaking.

I did not get to meet my first-born son until 6 hours later when they wheeled my bed up to the neonatal unit at around midnight. He was in an incubator hooked up to wires and machines and it was quite distressing to see. He looked so small and vulnerable and was black and blue with bruising to his body and his arm was splinted. He spent two weeks and a day in the special care baby unit. I was in hospital for 10 days following the birth. For the first 24 hours after the birth, I was hooked up to a morphine drip as I needed strong pain relief given what my body had gone through. This gave me hallucinations in the night which was quite scary. The whole experience of having my first born was very traumatic and only made better by the fact that we had a precious new baby we absolutely adored and couldn't wait to get him home.

We were not aware of any problems until he was around 14 months and he was not walking or trying to stand. He had been a bit slow to hit milestones and we mentioned this to our health visitor who referred us to see a community paediatrician. When we explained about Liam being premature and about his birth, he said that Liam was brain damaged and would need help with his learning and development and was referred to the physiotherapy department and the Early Years Teaching Team.

When we met the physiotherapist, we were told that Liam had Left Hemiplegia. We had no idea that it meant that he had a form of Cerebral Palsy. It wasn't until I looked it up on the internet that I fully understood what this meant. Liam had a weakness on his left side and the muscles in his left leg and foot were very tight. He had his leg and ankle stretched and put into plaster several times and following this he wore a foot splint. Liam started having regular physiotherapy sessions at home and we also went to a thera-play group (a physiotherapy session based around play activities) which encouraged him to stand and to walk. By Christmas 2004, four months after his 2nd birthday, he was walking!

Liam also had an early years teacher do weekly home visits up until he started school and speech and language input. He started school around a week after his 4th birthday and he never looked back! He always worked so hard at school and was like a sponge soaking it all up. He got stronger and fitter, wore insoles in his shoes to help with support and he just continued to thrive. He has achieved so much in his twenty years; he passed all his GCSE's and went on to get 4 A*'s in his A Levels. Although he has never been very sporty, he found that he enjoyed Archery and taking part in competitions and is now also a keen runner. We couldn't be prouder of what he has achieved and we often think back to what the community paediatrician said to us in the beginning that our son would have learning and physical problems! Well, I think he proved him more than wrong there!

In 2008 I became pregnant with our second child Sean. From the beginning, midwives and doctors were aware of my back condition and my previous pregnancy. I was monitored regularly and everything seemed to be going well so when I went into labour 9 weeks early on November 20th it was a huge shock. This time I was bleeding heavily; the placenta had ruptured. In case of a premature delivery, I was given a steroid injection to help with the prematurity of Sean's lungs but shortly after this, he seemed to be in distress so I was whisked into theatre to have an emergency Caesarean. I had explained to the nurse that when I had Liam, I didn't get to see him straightaway; he had been rushed off to PICU so she made sure that I got a glimpse of Sean before he too was rushed off to PICU. I couldn't believe this was happening again and I could not hold my baby.

Sean was in PICU for a week before being moved to another hospital's High Dependency Unit as at the time he was seen as the healthiest baby in the unit and PICU was so busy with babies with more complex needs. He spent a further 3 weeks there until he was discharged shortly before Christmas. In that time, he had a scan on his brain which is routine when a baby is born so premature and when we received the results, we received the news that Sean also had cerebral palsy but his condition was more severe. He was diagnosed as having Bilateral Periventricular Leukomalacia (PVL). The paediatrician was not sure how it would affect Sean but there was a good chance that all his limbs would be affected. As Sean would grow it would become more apparent what we were dealing with.

When Sean was 9 months old, he was diagnosed as having Epilepsy. We contacted his Paediatrician as he had been acting strangely. We would sit him on our lap and he would suddenly fling his arms out and scream like he was scared and then be calm again. This would come and go. The Paediatrician thought that he could be having seizure activity. Sean would cry a lot as a baby and it was hard to settle him. If we went out in the car and he was in his car seat he became very distressed unlike his older brother Liam who always fell asleep in the car as a baby! The same happened when we took him out in his pushchair.

We took him to have an EEG and shortly after the test, I received a phone call to bring him back to hospital to be admitted. It turned out the results of the EEG were so bad that he had to be put on steroids immediately. He was diagnosed with Epilepsy (West Syndrome). The electrical activity in his brain was so scrambled and it explained why Sean was so often distressed. He was in hospital for a couple of weeks and was put on medication to control the seizures he was having.

Shortly before his 1st birthday we went to the Opthalmology Department as we had concerns about Sean's vision. He was diagnosed as having a significant cortical or cerebral visual impairment and a convergent squint in both eyes. His problems with vision stem from problems with the nervous system and with the brain's ability to process messages sent from the eyes, not with the eyes themselves. We were put in touch with the charity VISTA. (*Vista are the leading local charity providing support for children and adults affected by sight loss*). They have provided us with important help and support with visual impairment over the years. We have enjoyed music therapy, trips and get togethers with parents of similarly affected children.

In 2012 we brought a Siberian Husky into our home and she has been a real tonic for the whole family. I'd had dogs all my life and we had recently lost a dog to old age so to bring home a new puppy was a delight and she has become a big part of the family. She gets us out and about in the fresh air which is great for our sanity, she has helped to pull Sean's wheelchair up some steep hills but not only that, she has sensed a couple of times when Sean is about to have a seizure. She is normally calm and quiet but there have been a few times when she will be sniffing Sean and will not leave him alone and shortly after this, he has had a seizure.

Sean is now 15 years old and is a very happy, cheeky young man. He attends a Special Needs school, is a wheelchair user and is fully dependent on adult support for all his needs. I'm so proud of both of my boys. They have both overcome so many struggles and have achieved so much in their own way. They have taught me so much. I feel stronger, more confident and resilient and that's probably in part due to the fact that we have had to fight at times to be heard. No-one will know your child better than you and you have to believe in that and make people listen which is hard at times. It has not been an easy experience being a parent to two children with cerebral palsy, having their own individual struggles, but it has been so rewarding. When they have achieved a goal, big or small, we have never taken it for granted, we have appreciated and taken joy in every moment.

It can be tough at times and some days are exhausting. You feel that you need to be fully alert and on par every day. You can't be ill and if you are, you have to keep going because no-one is going to step in and take over! Your own health is so important when you are caring for someone and they are fully reliant on you.

Little things like going out for the day or just for a walk to the park are not easy as there can be so many things that you have to remember to bring with you and there are not enough accessible changing places that have hoists and changing beds.

There seems to be a lack of activities and clubs for children with disabilities which can be very frustrating unlike for able bodied children.

One world can feel closed off to you but then another world opens up and we've met some wonderful people over the years that we would never have met otherwise. We have enjoyed some special experiences with some brilliant charities that provide activities and experiences for children with special needs. We feel very lucky to have had the opportunities that we have been given and have some wonderful memories.

Mummy knows best

By Kathryn Anne Sankey (Marshall)

Kathryn is 33 years old and lives in Middlesbrough, with her little girl Lola, age 6. She was a chef prior to having Lola and has also lived in Cyprus (Paphos) for a good few years as a teen. Lola is home schooled due to multiple safeguarding issues and they are now 6 months in and thriving!

They enjoy getting out and about exploring high-energy activities and in particular their local trampoline park.

Mummy knows best

I should have known that throwing up over 100 times a day was the start of things to come.
Hyperemesis -the devil!

Hospital admissions twice weekly were just awful; I felt like I had nothing left in my body to give to this little bump. Lola was delivered early by induction at 37 weeks due to low blood flow to the cord and no weight gain in 2 weeks.
Lola was born weighing just 5lb.

As a first time mum I thought 'that's it, she's in the world - my worries are over'. As a matter of fact, this is when things went anything but straight forward. We stayed for 47 nights after Lola was born in the local hospital for one reason or another. Lola struggled to feed as a newborn and was diagnosed with CMPA (cow's milk protein allergy) and was on a formula that smelt like a mouldy wash basket called Neocate.

We noticed, at around 5 months old, Lola wasn't like other children; she would react differently to sounds, lights, people and other stimuli.
I remember taking her to a local music class for babies. I was looking around with tears flooding my eyes; why is nobody else's baby doing what mine is doing?! I left the group that day broken and I poured my heart out to my husband.
Why is she not like other children?
Have I done something wrong?
I then begged my husband to use our savings to have Lola assessed by an occupational therapist. We did this, and I can honestly say it was our saving grace.
I felt less crazy. Less anxious.
And I felt like I was listened to.

Lola received a diagnosis of Sensory Processing Disorder and we then pushed the GP to refer her to a paediatrician with the evidence we had. Our health visitor told me that I should seek help for Post Natal Depression when actually was there was nothing wrong with me. Naturally, I was just a worried Mum!

We were left to wait a very long time before seeing someone qualified. It felt like a lifetime. Upon entering the room, I was desperately seeking some kind of confirmation that I wasn't crazy and our little lady would grow healthy and happy. We were put into the MAAT pathway for an Autism diagnosis and received this on Lola's 3rd birthday. We were literally diagnosed and given a leaflet. The support post-diagnosis was non-existent in my area. My husband and I felt almost grief after diagnosis.
Why us?
Why our little girl?
She is now diagnosed with Sensory Processing Disorder , Autism Spectrum Disorder, PICA / absence seizures - the list unfortunately goes on.

We had so many questions about the future, getting the right support and working out how we make her life as beautiful as possible.

Lola is now age 6. After multiple attempts at SEN provisions for Lola had failed, she is now home-schooled. She is thriving not just surviving. Not one size fits all and my best advice to any parent going through what we did was to get early intervention.

The process to get help and a diagnosis is just far too long in the UK. The sooner that ball starts rolling the better. I would also say find your village! Get out to some groups for kids the same as yours and meet other parents going through the same. I've had far superior support from others going through similar experiences, compared to the professionals. Our children are different yes, but these kids are given to strong amazing parents and don't ever forget that's what you are.

We are superheroes without the capes and bags under our eyes instead.

Keep going.

Keep pushing.

Keep ringing the services to chase up appointments.

And always remember yes, our hands are well and truly full
But our hearts are fuller.

Living in a whirlwind

By Jenni Jolly

Jenni Jolly is a mum & carer for her son and daughter who both have additional needs. They both have various different diagnoses. Jenni lives with her husband, four children and various pets in East Lothain, Scotland.

Living in a whirlwind

At 20yrs old I was told I could never have children. Shortly after marrying my husband, in order to get the family we wanted, we had to undergo fertility treatment. We were lucky to be blessed with 3 boys.

When I fell pregnant with Reuben, I knew it would be a difficult pregnancy because with my other boys I developed Hyperemesis which is a severe form of sickness that lasted until the day I gave birth. To survive I had to take a strong combination of anti-sickness drugs that are normally given to patients undergoing chemotherapy. We had extra scans to make sure he was growing ok and there were no signs that we would be embarking on a different journey than expected. His birth was long & difficult. When he was laid on my chest, I can remember my husband saying, "Is he ok?" as he was grey, not making a sound. It was only when he spoke up that the midwife yelled at him to press the emergency alarm and the next thing we knew, another doctor came running in and took our baby to another room. A very long 20 minutes later he was brought back to me, and we were told everything was fine. Imagine our surprise to be told to go home 6 hrs later without any checks by the consultant that all babies are supposed to get. They said they were too busy and that we would get an appointment in the post to come back to have the checks done. So, at 10pm that night, we left with our newborn to go home. The very next day the midwife was so shocked that our son hadn't been checked over that she called the hospital there and then and demanded that we were given an appointment that day. The hospital said everything seemed ok.

Over the coming weeks, I thought his head looked a bit bigger than normal, but everyone said he was fine. It wasn't until when he was 6 weeks old that a Santa hat that I had bought 3 weeks before that was too big for him was now far too small. My husband agreed that something wasn't right, so I contacted my health visitor as we were due our 6-week check-up anyway but I got told I had to be patient and wait for the appointment. That appointment didn't come till he was 11 weeks old. I can remember sitting in the waiting room, cradling my son and a woman came to sit next to us with her baby. She asked me how old my son was and when I said 11 weeks she said her baby was the same age. I remember looking at her baby and thinking "Wow he can hold his head," and it was then that the doubt started to creep in making me think that there could be something wrong. We were called in and went through the usual chat about everything and she then asked if I had any concerns. I explained about his head size, and she asked me to put Reuben on the bed and she would examine him. I watched her face go from smiling to frowning. She looked at me and said that she needed to get a GP. The GP explained she was very concerned and was putting an urgent referral to the hospital. This is when our journey started.

We met with Reuben's paediatrician who wanted to know everything about the fertility treatment we went through to get pregnant, what my pregnancy was like, and the birth. Lots of medical tests were ordered and referrals made to other departments. She gently explained that our son was significantly delayed and showed signs of a genetic syndrome.

The first 2 years of his life were a whirlwind of various medical tests which always came back normal or abnormal but with no explanation as to why it was abnormal. It was a very lonely time as we didn't really belong anywhere. As we had no overall diagnosis, there was very little support available to us until he was 2 years old and the paediatrician referred him to a SEN nursery. The support from them was amazing and we also started attending a SEN playgroup which was much easier than the normal mum and baby groups as I always felt left out seeing their children develop, sit and crawl around while mine was still like a newborn at 8 months old. We also got an amazing health nurse who worked as a liaison between the health visitors and the paediatrician & it's thanks to her that we got all the support we needed with Reuben. She helped us to get referred to the disability team when he was 2 years old and since then we have been supported by them and continue to do so now.

When Reuben was 18 months old I was told about a support network, SWAN UK (run by the charity Genetic Alliance UK) who support families whose children don't have a diagnosis. They have been a lifeline and I have made many friends through them. We no longer feel alone, it's comforting knowing there are other families who understand what our life is like.

We have had many challenges especially with education. The Local Authority said he was to go to a mainstream school with only 10 hours of support a week. No matter how I insisted it wasn't enough, they were adamant that they knew best. Luckily the school he went to was amazing and by the end of his first week, they knew he needed a full time 1:1, which he got. The school gave him an individualised timetable and supported him in everything, but as the years passed, we could see the gap getting wider and they recommended asking the Local Authority to move him to a SEN school full-time. We were turned down because he could speak a few words! Unbelievable! But the Local Authority then said he was to spend half the day in mainstream and the other half in an SEN school. It soon became apparent that he was thriving in the SEN environment so back to panel we went to ask the Local Authority to move him. Thankfully they saw sense and he was finally moved to an SEN school full time at 10 years old.

Reuben is now 13 years old and has a list of diagnoses like Epilepsy, significant learning disabilities, ASD, tremors, white matter changes on his brain, but still has no overall diagnosis despite all the genetic tests. He does have a mutation on one gene, but as he is the only one in the world with it, our doctors won't consider it as a diagnosis, so in the meantime they treat all the other diagnoses, and we have to wait for genetic tests to advance more before doing any more testing. It has not been an easy journey as we had to fight for the right support, fight to get him the right education he deserves, fight to even get him the medical treatment he deserves. Just because he is unable to communicate, doesn't mean he can be left at the bottom of a pile. He is important just like any other child and deserves to be treated as such.

We always said that our family was complete after Reuben was born and when we discovered he had severe complex needs we were glad he was our last. Little did we know what was in store for us.

When Reuben was 5 years old, I discovered I was pregnant with our little miracle as after all those years of trying and enduring fertility treatment I somehow ended up falling pregnant naturally! After the shock we were happy but then we started worrying about whether the baby would have the same needs as Reuben, would we be able to cope with another disabled child? I spoke to his paediatrician who immediately contacted the genetic team to discuss the risks of this pregnancy. At 20 weeks pregnant we met with the genetic team who basically said that as Reuben had no overall diagnosis there was no way of them knowing if this baby would also have issues. They did however say as we already had 2 older children who were healthy with no issues that our chances were very slim in having another child with a disability.

We spent the rest of the pregnancy worrying and thinking all sorts of scenarios. I also had Hyperemesis again so was on strong medication along with a pair of crutches as I developed severe SPD. I had to be induced as they were worried the baby was too big and the fact that I was so ill with being sick all day long and unable to walk without crutches. She came into the world screaming - the only one of my kids to do so, and when she was weighed, I can remember the midwife saying to me "No wonder you screamed so much, she is 10lb 2oz!" When Faith was born all seemed fine, she however failed her newborn screening, but I wasn't worried as all my boys failed theirs and when they were retested, they had passed so we thought the same would happen with Faith. Yet when we returned 2 weeks later I was devastated to be told that Faith had a profound hearing loss in both ears. My husband and I are both deaf but as we had 3 hearing boys, we assumed Faith would be hearing too so it was a shock to find out she was deaf too. I think I was so upset because I knew how hard it would be for her growing up.

Then at her 6 week check-up, the GP raised some concerns and asked for Reuben's paediatrician to examine her. It confirmed she had a developmental delay but that she wasn't too worried as Faith presented differently to how Reuben did at her age which was reassuring but at the same time worrying. We were referred to genetics and the community child health.

The first year of Faith's life was just a whirlwind of emotions, of constant appointments, many medical tests and juggling family life with 3 boys, one with complex needs. Every single week that year we had an appointment for either one of them and it was very overwhelming.

Faith was diagnosed with Waardenburg Syndrome which caused her deafness. It's a rare syndrome and comes with some various symptoms some of which Faith had. I discovered that she had inherited it from me as this was the reason I was deaf too and I never knew. I had a lot of guilt in knowing it was me who passed the gene in causing her deafness. But my husband gently reminded me that we would be the best role models for her and we would know what she would need in order to cope in a hearing world. We made the decision to have her bilaterally implanted so that she could have the best of both worlds – deaf and hearing. Faith's first language is BSL – British Sign Language just like her brothers before they learned to speak and once she was implanted, she then developed speech. Now she is fluent in both. However, we noticed Faith wouldn't talk or sign in front of other people, not even to other family members. At nursery, she never made a sound and was so shy. Her speech therapist sat me down and asked me if I knew what Selective Mutism was. Faith was officially diagnosed with it at 3 years old. I made the decision to enrol her in the same school as Reuben due to how amazing the school was in supporting us and Reuben with his additional needs. Thankfully she got a place there and with the help of her teacher of the deaf, she soon settled and became happy there. The school learned all about selective mutism and received deaf awareness training which helped them to know what the best way was to support her and include her in school life.

The first 2 years flew by with very few issues but we started noticing some traits in her, how she had difficulties with certain things, how much she needed to know and understand things before they happened, how she liked routine, and how much she struggled after school with huge meltdowns. One of the learning disability team who worked with Reuben actually suggested to me that I should get her assessed for Autism. I was taken back, and I did the only thing I could cope with at the time which was to bury my head in the sand. I tried to convince myself that as school saw no issues that meant she was fine. How wrong was I?

After a hard summer break dealing with constant meltdowns from both younger ones, being stuck in the house as I was unable to take them both out myself, I was looking forward to the school routine and getting some time to be able to just sit and have a hot cuppa tea without any chaos! But this is when everything changed. Faith had an appointment with her paediatrician as her speech therapist was worried about how bad her anxiety had become along with concerns with eating etc. The paediatrician recommended that she be referred for possible assessment for ASD / ADHD which was hard to hear. Once school term started, Faith started saying she was unwell, started getting upset in the mornings, becoming anxious about many things and it escalated to the point where she was unable to go into school.

Gone was the happy, funny, cheeky little girl that I knew, she became very anxious, worried about everything, emotional, meltdowns, violence, no interest in her toys, no interest in her hobbies. Instead, she clung to me, watched videos on her tablet, didn't want to go out and shut herself off from us.

Meetings were held, lots of discussions were had to try to get to the bottom of it all and we discovered how much Faith was masking, how much she was struggling with all the changes in school, how she was struggling with schoolwork etc. We now have a lot more adult support in place, and interventions inside the classroom and school to help her. Visuals have helped us to understand her emotions better as she struggles to verbalise at times so having this in place has helped me to understand what is going on in her head. Now it's just a waiting game to have her assessed which sadly can take years. I'm so thankful for her school and her teacher of the deaf who have gone above and beyond in ensuring my girl is supported.

I have struggled a lot the past few months in trying to accept that I have 2 children with additional needs who are both very similar but yet so different in many ways. They both have taught me to slow down and appreciate the small things, to celebrate the inch stones instead of worrying about the big milestones. Their smiles and laughter light up the darkest days.

They both have their own unique path and I, along with my husband, will be behind them every step of the way making sure they get every support they need in life.

Our SonShine

By Mary Liquorish (Mazz)

Mazz (Mary) Liquorish has a husband, 3 daughters, 1 son (James-15) (pictured), 1 stepson, 3 granddaughters, and a dog called Billy.
She is a full-time carer for James, and she works from home baking personalised shortbread biscuits in her spare time. Before James's diagnoses, she owned her own cafe business - she gave up her cafe to free up time to care for James.
In her spare time, she loves to knit, crochet, sew, bake, go to bingo, eat out, and she loves to go to the theatre and cinema. Mazz is very creative and enjoys concocting new ideas; she loves spending time with her family and friends. She particularly loves spending quality time with James.

Our SonShine

When my husband, Darren, and I first met it was clear from the start that we were two people who were meant to be one! We were so happy to have found each other! Soon after, we got some exciting news "We were having a baby...a baby BOY." After having 3 daughters already, you can imagine how excited I was!! Our son James was born on September 20th 2008, a beautiful healthy baby! "Or so we thought!"

For the first couple of years, James seemed absolutely fine, a bit delayed in his motor development but that didn't worry us too much. Having already had children, we knew they all developed in their own time! When James was about 2 and a half years old, he was showing some signs of weakness. At first, we noticed a twist in his ankle and a slight waddle when he walked. We thought this may have something to do with his delayed development so we took him to the doctors who referred him to the children's outpatients at Leicester Royal Infirmary (LRI). After being examined, they diagnosed James with flat feet and hyper mobility (double jointed).

When James was 3 and a half, we as parents still felt something wasn't quite right, so off we went back to the doctors, who then referred us back to the LRI. This time James had a blood sample taken along with another full examination! We were told his results would take up to 10 days. The very next morning we got a phone call from the hospital asking us to go back as his bloods had shown to be abnormal; they told us they suspected Muscular Dystrophy! We could not believe our ears!

We had to take James back for a second set of bloods and then a third for DNA! Eventually James had to have a muscle biopsy, which in May 2013 confirmed 'Duchenne Muscular Dystrophy.' As you can imagine, we were devastated! We felt helpless! And Disbelief! But we knew there was nothing we could do!
Not only did we have this devastating news, we also had the devastating news of my sister Sheila who passed away from cancer in July 2013!

It felt like we were living a nightmare!!
A year we would never forget!!

And after putting our wedding day off for 2 years because our daughter lost our grandson at the age of 3mths old, Darren and I Married on August 31st 2013.
A year of so many mixed feelings!

So.....what we thought we would do is turn a negative into a positive and concentrate on what we CAN DO - fundraise for research! Maybe one day soon they may find a cure, if not a cure, then better treatment to improve lives.

We started a fundraising team called Tri4james! We literally ploughed ourselves into raising as much as we could for various different charities, all hoping to improve the lives of people with Duchenne Muscular Dystrophy:

. 3x Triathlons
. An Open water swim
. 10x London Marathon
. A Walk from Leicester to Skegness
. A Fashion Show
. A shop fete
. Cake Sales galore
. Love Run
. Children's Sponsored Walk
. Leicester Half Marathon
. Derby 10k
. Park Runs galore
. Curry Night
. Barn Dance
. Head Shave
. Tough Mudder
. Various School fetes

- Go Orange Day (School)
- Bake a Difference
- Sky Dive
- Three-Legged Walk
- Bracelet Making
- Manchester relay Marathon

And many, many more.... We literally burnt out!!! It seemed endless!

Nothing we were doing seemed enough! We were missing out on valuable time with our boy, time that no amount of money could buy, so we decided to quit the fundraising and focus on JAMES.

We visited Australia - Adelaide and Sydney; James has also been lucky enough to visit Walt Disney World in Orlando Florida twice! We had a blast. Anywhere James wanted to go, we tried our best to purchase tickets! If we couldn't afford it, we would approach a charity who would help us fund it. James has also been privileged to meet so many celebrities, his favourite being Jamie Vardy from Leicester City's Football Team.

James is now 15yrs old, and doing quite well all things considered. It's been a rocky road to say the least, emotionally and physically draining, especially at the end of 2020, when James underwent open heart surgery to close a hole on his heart; he hasn't walked since. Despite the surgery going really well, he seemed to lose all his confidence. Since then, James is now a full time power wheelchair user. He seems happy most of the time but also says he just wants to do normal things like normal children of his age. He has three nieces who he sees enjoying life to the full, and although he's happy for them he also feels sad because he can't do what they can.

James is due to have Spinal Surgery in April this year and is feeling very anxious about the whole ordeal - we all are! This is to correct his Scoliosis; most boys with Duchenne get scoliosis at some point in their lives! This will give James a better posture, making him much more comfortable in his chair.

It's an Emotional Rollercoaster it really is!

I feel so saddened for James and yet I feel so lucky to have him in our lives, although I yearn for a life without Duchenne!

"DUCHENNE" IS NOT HIS NAME!

A poem by Mazz (Mary) Liquorish

Our SON has this condition,
DUCHENNE is its name,
He gets a little tired,
And his muscles are to blame.

His day can be quite challenging,
But every day he tries his best,
He could walk and run and jump,
Although not as fast as all the rest.

Our family and friends encourage him,
To always try his best,
When he gets a little tired,
His body has to rest.

Sometimes when he fell over,
And he ended up on the floor,
He got himself back on his feet,
And tried a little more.

He dreamt of being like Spiderman,
Or maybe even Hulk!
But because he didn't have super powers,
He sometimes sat to sulk.

Then he quickly reminded himself,
He was SUPER just the same,
His muscles may have been weaker,
But he had a lot to gain.

He loved to play some football,
Even though he wasn't that strong,
He kicked the ball towards the net,
And he sometimes got it wrong,

In his mind he was running fast,
In his mind he was kicking high,
In his mind he is no different,
He could even learn to fly.

You see, just because he's weaker,
He's still the same as you,
He too has hopes and dreams,
That one day may come true.

So...we're going to enjoy his life,
As best as we know how,
We will do the things he likes to do,
We'll find a way somehow.

Although...he relies more now on his power-chair
As his condition takes its toll,
But that's ok, he feels safer there,
He feels in control.

So when he's sitting in his power-chair,
to take himself to school,
He has his independence,
Which makes him feel really cool.

Please try not to treat him differently,
He's the same as all of you,
Just ever so slightly weaker,
and a little slower too.

Please always walk beside him,
and he will ride beside you,
and if you decide to be his friend,
He may decide to be yours too.

Then you can teach each other,
that your lives are just the same,
He may have this condition but.......

"JAMES LIQUORISH"
"IS HIS NAME!" X

More than a statistic

By Nichola Kerr

Nichola Kerr is a care-experienced teen mother, an AUDHD adult, qualified counsellor, a parent panel member of the family rights group, a now second-time nanny of two beautiful granddaughters and a parent carer of 4 autistic daughters. A resident of the northwest of England with her two youngest daughters, her Husband and 3 fur babies with her inner circle of family living not far. Many would describe her as a amazing friend, a witty woman, and a loving mother. She is also a "published author" in Free loaves on Fridays and she uses her experience to encourage others.

More than a statistic

My journey to parenthood was different to many others. I was a teen when I got pregnant with my eldest daughter and was in the care system. Before conceiving my child, I was in a mental health facility for adolescents. I was there for around 6 months. I was deemed a danger to myself and others. I suffered with PTSD, Depression, Anxiety, self-harming and risky behaviours. Looking back, I was lucky to have a good social worker that helped get me the support I needed the most, although I didn't see it at the time. I had no family or friends to support me. I had no home and no stability. My baby changed my life. She gave me a reason to keep going. I had to fight to keep my baby.

Pregnancy with my first born was unremarkable, apart from maybe the blood test at 12 weeks. I was given the news there were high markers for Down Syndrome and I was advised to have the amniocentesis done. I refused this due to the risk of miscarriage. Doctors and social workers were concerned about my ability to parent any child let alone a child with additional needs. So the recommendation was to end the pregnancy. I did not consider this as a personal option, so I continued my pregnancy. Throughout the pregnancy I feared health checks as the judgment was consistent. It was unsupportive and scary. The same conversations about how I wouldn't cope. I was 16 and alone, had no money, no home to call my own and a history of poor mental health. The people who said they were there to support me had only made me feel as though I had already failed at motherhood. The midwives felt cold and cruel constantly pressuring me to end my baby's life because I was incompetent for not wanting to take a test due to my risk of miscarriage. I was made to feel like my past struggles meant I was not of sound mind to make decisions for my baby and that I was going to subject her to the abuse and mistreatment I had suffered. They did this with no reason too. I was unfairly judged due to my age. So, I missed several appointments with the midwife in the early months and would only attend hospital if my baby had not moved. I would count the movements; I would drink cold water and have a bath. Everything to encourage my baby to move, nothing worked. At the hospital, the second the monitor came on, my baby would dance. I went to work in a taxi office to get money so I could provide for my child; the life I felt I was never worthy of and a life she could look back on and be proud of. I had a lot to prove.

As my pregnancy progressed, I was still a child of the system, they had concerns for my unborn child and a child protection order was requested. I was 16 and mostly alone. I attended the CP meetings and made agreements to engage with health and social care. They arranged a flat for me in a sheltered accommodation and in time I gave birth to my first baby, after 18 hours of labour, 3 days after my 17th birthday. She was perfect. Their test was wrong. At 18, social care left us as I had proven that I was a capable and loving parent and could keep my baby safe. I had reconnected with my birth family and was met with support and challenges. My baby was quiet and smart; we always stayed together which I was told was the reason she struggled to make friends. Nursery was amazing for her, she was supported and loved it. She thrived because of the unchanging stable routine it provided. She went to primary school and the difficulties started as she was not understood or supported. There were instances of bullying because she was strict with herself about following rules and the other children saw this as something to bully her about. This happened in the way of shoving and other physical taunting. School and health visitors didn't see any issues. At home she had her favourite videos to watch several times a day, every day. Despite having a wide selection of clothes in her wardrobe, she had a small selection of clothing that she could wear and her days were predictable. If things weren't predictable, she would become upset. She would not speak to people she didn't regularly see and this included her family, some of which she lived with. She was labelled as a picky eater. The health visitor said "She will grow out of it." When I raised my concerns, they took this as an opportunity to attack my parenting, telling me she must socialise more. This was impossible as I was shunned from parenting groups because I was a young single mother.

I went on to have another baby, again my pregnancy was unremarkable. I refused the blood test for the markers of Down Syndrome which remained the same with my future pregnancies because it would not have mattered to me either way. Single parent again and engaged in all of my medical appointments. I gave birth to my second baby at 22. My baby's delivery was difficult as her shoulder was stuck under my pelvis, she needed the Special Care Baby Unit (SCBU) now known as the NICU for 24 hours. She suffered with kidney problems, clicky hips and a dislocated shoulder as well as the fact she was unable to breathe without intervention and she was not eating. I was kept from my baby for 14 excruciating hours. These hours were not difficult because of my physical injuries but rather because all I had of my baby was a picture.

Behaviour wise, she was the polar opposite to my first born; where my first born was calm and placid my second born was hyperactive, wouldn't sleep and needed constant stimulation and activity.

By age 3, she was dressing herself in clothes she had chosen and was absconding out the front door to play with friends in the street. I locked doors but she'd climb out the windows. She was in and out of hospital with injuries. One time she pulled a wardrobe and TV onto herself, another time we were playing in the shop and she pulled away and her elbow popped out. It was hard work. The school and health visitor didn't identify any issues with her.

I went on to have another 2 children, both born by C section due to the complicated birth of no 2. Both pregnancies were unremarkable. I had a partner now and we married. I was mid 20s so the judgment was not present, and I had support from him and his family. My Mum was still very supportive and present.

We recognised the same difficulties presented with all 4 of them. Mental health, low mood, difficulty with friendships, eating difficulties, fighting, unable to attend school were a few of the things we recognised at first. Over the years we have asked schools for help, LA for help, family for help. It has always been the same outcome. It is your parenting; it is your mental health that is causing your children's poor mental health. I was asked the question, "Is the reason you fight so hard for your children because nobody fought for you," when the real reason I fought so hard is because I am a mother who loves her children. "We don't see anything at school, she's copying her sister, she's copying you." So many people kept telling me it was my parenting. Every assessment when we asked for help we were directed towards parenting courses and parenting assessments whereby I'd have to relive my own upbringing and be judged again. Blamed for my children's difficulties again. Retraumatised again.

It was my eldest daughter that recognised my children's difficulties and used the term Autism to describe the difficulties they were having. She was in her final year of A levels in college for child development. I dismissed it as this is surely something that would be identified by all of the professionals that we had seen.

She went on to university to study educational psychology and came home and said again, they are Autistic. We embarked on our own learning about Autism and ADHD.

Schools dismissed us, doctors dismissed us because school didn't see anything, in meetings they told us that they were copying each other and social care blamed my parenting.

One by one, our children started getting diagnosed. It started with an ADHD diagnosis for child No 2. Then the Autism diagnosis started and now all 4 of them are diagnosed Autistic. My youngest two children are still in education; their views and opinions have been dismissed. They have been bullied, they have been traumatised through an education system that has built-in exclusion for people who do not fit the mould. They have lost trust in professionals. They have missed out on years of education and an opportunity to socialise. My 3rd child who is at GCSE level is only now learning Maths. After years of being too "dumb" to learn, she is now ghost writing these pages of my story. My 4th baby is now exploring EOTAS and inspiring all of us on her journey of self-exploration and representation.

I received my ADHD validation 2 years ago and I'm waiting for my Autism validation.

The hardest part of this journey has not been parenting my children it has been the dismissal of their difficulties and the lack of support and encouragement they have had. The hardest part for me of being a parent carer is the negativity, prejudice, judgement and bullying they have experienced and continue to experience for being who they are. As a parent carer, I have been dismissed, gaslit, blamed and threatened with further social care involvement. Accused of not meeting needs, threatened with school fines and threatened by police for protecting my child in our home.

The highest part of my journey is having the absolute privilege to be a part of their lives and their journeys into themselves. To watch them grow and develop into the people they were always meant to become.

My hope for them is that they keep following their path, keep believing in themselves and I hope they know how very proud I am of every one of them.

They have taught me that I have a voice, through them needing me to advocate for them, they have taught me how to be me and not apologise for being me.

A final message to any parent carer: You are the expert of your child. You are their safe person. Advocate for them, reach out to the parent carer community or create your own. This is not a solo journey, and it is a journey, not a destination.

Misunderstood

By Eleanor Wheatley

Eleanor Wheatley is a Mum, trained originally as a Dental Technician and now works as a Learning Support Assistant. She is a carer to her 3 children. A 14-year-old Boy who is Autistic, Dyslexic and Dysgraphic, an 11-year-old boy who is Autistic and has a Tic disorder and an 8-year-old girl who is Autistic. Eleanor lives with her husband and 3 children in Leicestershire, England.

Misunderstood

To explain our story never feels like a simple task. It often feels like one of those films where they are telling several stories simultaneously, that somehow eventually intertwine and make sense. Through understanding there was something different to my children's path, I was likewise able to make sense and understand why my own had been somewhat challenging. Because of the challenges I faced growing up, I was perhaps more mindful when my eldest son was developing a little differently to his peers. For many years though I was assured that this was likely to him being a summer born boy. Things like his speech, coordination, the way he played, hitting milestones like walking just that bit later. I believed quite early on that there was maybe a learning difficulty that was playing a part in this and wanting the very best start for him, I expressed my concerns to our GP who was quite dismissive over taking these any further. Thankfully at this point he was still under the health visitor who did listen and support a referral to the community paediatrician. At the time, one of my nieces had been diagnosed with Dyspraxia and I felt this may likely be the case for my son, lots of the early signs were present and so it made sense.

In my own story I struggled to learn at the same pace as my peers, but it didn't end there as I was equally different at home. As a child I felt a great sense of shame every time I couldn't understand the work that my peers seemed to grasp with ease, until I eventually assumed my position as just a failure - but I didn't fail. My path just had a lot more bends in the road then others. I learnt a different way. I eventually left school with all of my GCSE's despite doing nothing to revise for them. Granted all C's and D's but it left me with this question - what could I have achieved had my alternate way of thinking been understood? Had a logical explanation been given, that was more than me just not being good enough? Had just any one of my teachers believed that I was more - I wonder still.

I naively believed that finding the answers for my children would mean they would get the support that was needed when starting school, particularly given that my eldest would only just have turned 4 when this was to happen and like most learning differences, the importance of early intervention is often emphasised.

When we eventually saw the community paediatrician, signs of Dyspraxia were acknowledged but no suggestion of any other possibilities. I look back now at conversations I had with numerous professionals and wonder how certain behaviours I had mentioned (like the lining and organising of his toys) was so easily dismissed. He loved to play with soldiers; he would spend significant chunks of time organising them and this was deemed what little boys do. The realisation that perhaps there could be another answer only came to my attention a couple of years later through a program that I just happened to watch - 'Born naughty'. Now by no means at all was my son a child that was ever considered "naughty", in fact he was always quite the opposite. However, one child displayed some similar behaviours to him, lining things up, responding differently to hugs, appearing to not hear despite passing hearing tests, fixed interests to name a few. At the end of the program various professionals gave the child a diagnosis of Autism. This was the pivotal moment for our family, the lightbulb moment that started the chain of events, where eventually all 3 of my children were diagnosed and I most recently have joined the pathway searching for answers. The answer as they say is often right under your nose and in my case the answers I had long searched for had been there all along, but this was not understood. It leaves me wondering again though, had I not found the answer would we be where we are today? How many families will never know? Though I see this now as the moment starting this chain of events, this doesn't mean however that to get to the place we are today has been easy. Many people shut down or laughed at the possibility that my eldest particularly was Autistic. Although I have not been immune to this scepticism with my younger children in their early years, once they started primary school I was fortunate that the SENCO (more recent addition to the school at the time) took the time to listen, acknowledge and support my concerns. There were of course a lot of people along the way who could have easily dissuaded me, people who simply did not have the understanding or experience to do so;

"Children with Autism will behave the same in all situations. They wouldn't be able to hide their struggles."

"I have been told that families with more than one child diagnosed, it's because of poor parenting."

"No, I've worked with Autistic children before. X is definitely not Autistic."

"They are just copying behaviours from their siblings."

"He's just a summer born boy."

This left our path to discovery a lot harder, I felt I needed evidence to prove what I was seeing. Videos, photographs so people would understand that what I was saying was really happening. When we were seen again by the community paediatrician for our eldest, we were given GARS 2 forms to fill in. One for us and one for school. Now our form gave strong suggestion of Autism, however schools did not and our word alone was not enough for the paediatrician to agree. Referrals were made to SALT and occupational therapy for a neurodevelopmental sensory screen, which along with a conclusive educational psychology report confirmed my suspicions. My son was diagnosed with Autism and Sensory Processing Disorder, but this took time. The experience left me guarded. There were few I trusted to confide in when things became challenging. None to understand, however well intentioned, when I felt like I was drowning, surrounded by people completely oblivious to the fact that things weren't ok. There were of course also times where I have desperately reached out for support from services that had been rejected. My son was in year 3 the first time he told me he wanted to die, to stab himself with a sharp knife and die because the school system left him feeling worthless. There are simply no parenting books in existence that can prepare you for this. We were referred on three separate occasions for support with his mental health. Every time we were advised they could not accept him onto their waiting list as it was a school issue and to hide our medicine and knives. Every time my children's hearts have broken because they couldn't cope. Those times where the struggle has broken their spirits. My heart has broken too. I wished they could see themselves through my eyes as I am honestly in awe of everything they are. We are open in our house about their being Autistic and encourage them to see this as a strength, for every change and innovation in life has come from someone with a different perspective. A different way of seeing the world.

I have found what support I could through Facebook pages for parents and carers of Autistic children. The anonymity helped, I have always been conscious that these are my children's truths to tell should they wish and I felt somewhere where nobody knew us was a way to respect that. I felt a great sense at last that we were all in it together, people who understood and wanted to support each other. I found myself reading through many posts; it taught me so much and it also led me to means of support I wasn't aware of, be it financial, support for us as family and trips supported by charities such as Miracles To Believe In. It helped me in the long run finding the right contacts and means to fight for what my children needed. Generally speaking, whatever we were going through, there was someone who understood and had been through it too and even when no one had, I still saw people supporting and pulling each other up.

When my eldest son was in year 5, he was assessed for an EHCP. As a result of the application, he was once again seen by the educational psychologist who also screened for Dyslexia. He had always struggled with reading and his writing was illegible. Through this screening, more areas of need were acknowledged - Dyslexia and Dysgraphia. Now Dyslexia I had some knowledge of, but I would be lying if I said that I had any clue what Dysgraphia was. With all this in mind my son was awarded an EHCP which was a great relief as despite having incredible knowledge within his special interest of History, he was working significantly behind his peers. Where we live, the high schools are heavily oversubscribed and this also gave us more control over where he went next, rather than leaving it to chance and at this point we hadn't really considered a specialist high school. He had managed through primary school to make and maintain a big group of friends, most of which would be going to the same high school. When the time came for open evenings, we noticed that he was unable to cope with the volumes of people and the size of the change. He shut down and we had to leave every school we attended, even when we visited out of hours with minimal staff and no pupils in sight; it was too much and he couldn't cope. When people spoke to him, he shut them out and couldn't respond. This was even the case within the specialist provision that we had decided to explore as an option. We were always stuck in a conundrum with him as he desperately needed support but was very against standing out and accepting it. There was a specialist school for those with moderate learning difficulties close by that had the feel of a high school but with much smaller class numbers and more support within the classroom so that he wouldn't stand out. It is here that we decided to name for our parental preference, but this decision was not by any means easy. There were elements that left us unsure of the right path for him as every option had something missing. Yes, he was working below expected levels but in other aspects he showed amazing potential, He had an amazing head for facts and was fantastic at strategic games like Risk or Chess. We always felt that his case has never been lack of ability but simply he needed a different approach. I chased relentlessly with our SENA case worker for an update to eventually find the consultation was missed by our chosen school and the local high school that his friends would attend responded saying they could "meet his needs." All the places had been allocated with the extras they were forced to take at the specialist provision we had settled on and so the mainstream high was named. We had been on the fence for a long time over which way was the best fit and he was keen to join his friends, so we eventually agreed to give him that chance. We had noticed from activities outside of school that he was increasingly uncomfortable with new people and we felt being supported by a group of friends would help this transition. Circumstances were not in his favour as he started at high school the Autumn term of 2020, COVID year with no transition which certainly wasn't the best start. He managed just short of a year and a half there before an independent, specialist placement was agreed where he is now thriving. There were however good and bad things to take from this. The school turned out to be particularly poor with SEND, despite going up with the full hours in support he was not receiving this. He was legally entitled to support stated in his plan, and when I reported this to SENA, I was pushed from pillar to post and no one as much as investigated my concerns. The school were not prepared to make reasonable adjustments and no one was prepared to help make sure his rights were enforced. His overall mental health rock bottomed and attendance was dropping. Despite this not being a school that I would recommend to anyone in our situation, despite all his struggles, he did develop many new friendships that he still maintains today, and that is a true testament to who he is as a person.

My eldest often refers to himself as the first pancake and much that I feel deeply saddened that this is how he sees it, it isn't an altogether inaccurate way to describe the situation. Not because he has turned out badly, quite the opposite. This is simply because there were things I learnt through this experience to do better. I can't help but wish now that I could go back and know then what I know now, but I had to learn through fighting for what was needed. This helped to a degree when requesting a specialist setting for our middle child, but it would be deceiving to say that this went without a hitch. I did however have more faith in myself, that I could get the job done. It taught me exactly what I was fighting for and I knew from this experience without question what was needed for them to succeed. I understand the system better. I wish he didn't go through the time he did, that his journey was simpler but I believe it meant we secured the perfect place for him and I love seeing his amazing personality now shining through. He has shown great strength, incredible wit, confidence and perseverance. Through it all he has always worked hard and has never quit!

We now have 2 of our children in a specialist school and the difference to their wellbeing, confidence and what they have been able to achieve has been incredible. They are much happier as they are accepted, understood and within an environment which they can thrive. We are starting the process to request for a specialist school for our daughter who is Autistic and situationally mute. Despite support from an amazing LSA, she is but a shadow of herself in her current setting and unable to access the learning. Although I have talked mainly about my eldest son that is not to say that I haven't faced many challenges with my other children, but his story was the one that opened the door to us all.

Things may not always go smoothly, we may not win every battle. I may not always get things right but I will try. Whatever it is, the highs or the lows, to quote Andre Day's song;

"I'll rise up
  I'll rise like the day
  I'll rise up
  I'll rise unafraid
  I'll rise up
  and I'll do it a thousand times again."

DDX3X: our journey to diagnosis and beyond

By Maria Poole

Maria Poole is a mum, editor, copy writer and primary carer of her 17-year-old daughter who has DDX3X syndrome. They live together in Bristol, UK.

DDX3X: our journey to diagnosis and beyond

Our daughter Alex got into the system at an early age. We noticed that she was developing much more slowly than the other babies we knew, for example they were all crawling whilst she still needed support to sit up. Every milestone was delayed. She didn't start to walk until she was just over two years. When she was about 18 months old, I took her to our GP and asked if I should be worried that she wasn't talking yet when all the other children were. We were then referred to the midwife who referred us to a paediatrician and then we were in!

The paediatrician referred us to Portage (a fantastic service) and also carried out an MRI and various genetic tests before diagnosing her with a Global Developmental Delay of unknown cause. We were also then referred to Physiotherapy, the Orthotics Service, Occupational Therapy, Speech and Language Therapy, the Community Learning Disability Nursing Service and Ophthalmology, so we certainly weren't short of services in those early years. Alex was further diagnosed with a Sensory Processing Disorder, proprioceptive difficulties, speech and language and fine and gross motor difficulties, autistic type traits around behaviour and communication and, more recently, a Cerebral Visual Impairment and extreme anxiety. The anxiety revolves around noises which are out of her control, starting in younger life with things like thunder, fireworks and fire alarms, it has now developed into a full-blown phobia of babies and small children crying. It worsened as she hit puberty and is, as you can imagine, immensely debilitating as babies and small children are everywhere! She becomes violent towards me or herself when she sees them. We now have involvement from a psychiatrist who is part of Learning Difficulties CAMHS.

As with all parents of disabled children we have faced many difficulties along the way and have had to fight tooth and nail to get Alex the services she needs, in and out of school. It seems to be standard practice in our Local Authority to discharge children from services like OT and SALT when they reach junior level. I guess a lack of staff and funding just doesn't allow them to carry on. Because of this, I funded a private OT to go into Alex's school for an hour a week to work with her. She's a sensory specialist so I was very lucky to find her. She's still involved in Alex's life now! Therapy wise I would say that Occupational therapy has had the most profound effect on my daughter's quality of life. Her 'sensory diet' can wake up or calm down her senses, enabling her to focus and concentrate.

Our paediatrician suggested the Deciphering Developmental Disorders (DDD) study to us when Alex was five. We said yes out of curiosity. We had no desperate desire at that stage to find out what was causing Alex's complex issues, but I felt that it might be of some use in retaining services when she was older. We were called by a counsellor from the hospital who went through the process with us on the phone and asked us various questions about our family and history. We then went to see a geneticist at the Bristol Children's Hospital. She talked us through everything and Alex went to have photos taken of various parts of her body. Then it was just a waiting game. We were told that we would find out within five years!

We received a diagnosis three years later when Alex was eight, she had a 'de novo' (spontaneous, not inherited) genetic mutation of the DDX3X gene. To be honest we'd just about given up on hearing anything by then and had mostly forgotten about it! Initially, when we first heard the results, I didn't feel that they had any significance for us personally as we were already so far down the road and had already fought for, and for the most part, put in place the help that Alex needed regardless of a pinpointed diagnosis. I thought that it would probably feel more important for parents with younger children. My only curiosity at first was if there was any possibility of knowing how Alex could develop in the future. As it turns out the children who are affected by the DDX3X mutation have varying extremes of symptoms depending on whereabouts on the DNA string the mutation has occurred. This means that it's impossible to track an individual path and predict the future. For example, some of the children have seizures and these can start from a young age or begin to occur when the child is a teenager, others not at all. Some children have no speech and there is a wide spectrum of intellectual disability. These are just a few examples of the differences which may occur. The DDX3X spectrum can range from severe to mild symptoms. I would say that Alex is on the mild to moderate end of that scale.

I was curious to meet parents who had children with the same mutation in the UK and I decided to start a UK Facebook page to find them. I found an American group which I also joined. Since then, I have started a patient group with a couple of other parents and the support of the Genetic Alliance, which has since been turned into a charity, DDX3X Support UK. The DDD diagnosis became important to us as it allowed us to create a supportive community. It's also empowering to know that in the future we can help other parents through the maze we've already negotiated and that, hopefully in the future we can encourage research into our children's particular syndrome.

I would like to say that we did feel somewhat cut adrift after receiving Alex's diagnosis via the DDD project. We saw the geneticist once at her clinic, and though she is happy to answer any queries which I might send to her (and is really helpful) there is currently no facility for multiple or yearly appointments to discuss any changes or new concerns. This is something that everyone in our Facebook group has mentioned. When your child has a rare condition, it feels that nobody is interested in it, or cares about it once they have been diagnosed. As most of the children have autistic traits, many of the parents try for that diagnosis simply to access help and support which is more readily available. So, I now think that a diagnosis is invaluable and it's worth the wait! What's lacking is support in place post diagnosis.

My daughter is now 17 and our next hurdle to negotiate is the transition to adult services, but I guess that will be a whole other story! We are also in the process of pursuing an Autism diagnosis as secondary to her genetic condition. Earlier in her life, I was aware that an Autism diagnosis could have led to diagnostic overshadowing with a risk of the pursuit of the root genetic cause of her condition then being abandoned. Now that she has been diagnosed with DDX3X syndrome, a Sensory Processing Disorder and a Cerebral Visual Impairment I feel that risk of overshadowing has lessened. It's extremely unlikely that Alex will ever live a fully independent life, so I'm hoping that the Autism diagnosis will help people to understand her better in adult life, especially around her behaviour and communication. Nobody's heard of DDX3X syndrome!

What's Alex like? Well, she's always been naturally sunny, bright and cheeky with a great sense of humour. She loves books and stories (listening to them and creating them, when she was smaller using small world characters and her imagination), watching DVDs, swimming, dancing, singing, writing and drawing. When Alex is happy, she is very chatty but quiet when overwhelmed. At primary level she attended a mainstream primary school with full time 1:1 but then transferred to a special school for her secondary education, and now attends a college for special needs which teaches foundation level skills. Though Alex has difficulties with communication, occasionally she amazes us with her understanding of language. For example, once when asked to describe a sports event at school she said that her friend 'ran like a lightning bolt'. On the other side of the coin her speech can be 'blurry' and difficult to understand at times.

My advice to any parents would be to become well informed about your child's condition, keep fighting and never give up. Also, make contact with other parents whose children have special needs; their support, advice and understanding will be invaluable to you as time goes on.

Information

The website for our charity is www.ddx3xsupportuk.co.uk
I wrote and designed the website so the picture on the home page is of Alex. You'll also find our family story on the site too.

Why me? Well my dear, why not?

By Fiona Williams

Fiona lives in Lincolnshire with her five children, four of whom have SEN needs from Leith with cerebral palsy, to his brothers with Autism and ADHD. She has got quite good at EHCPs and advocating for support and documents hers and her children's journey on Instagram at @survivingsen. If you are reading this and feel like you are drowning in grief and worry, just know you are not swimming alone, we can float together like otters.

Why me? Well my dear, why not?

Two blue lines. 14 week old baby. Two blue lines. 14 week old baby. As my eyes darted between the pregnancy test in my hand and my 14 week old baby in his bouncer by my feet, I cannot honestly say my first emotions were joyous. Fear, incredulity and shock dominated those first couple of weeks after finding out we were expecting our second son, along with the usual first trimester pregnancy symptoms and a couple of small bleeds, but eventually the excitement crept in and took over.

It was an easier pregnancy than my first, baby grew and at the 20 week scan we were told we would next be seen when baby was born, compared to the biweekly scans all the way through with my first baby. All seemed so simple and 'normal' - a word I have grown to hate over the past few years.

Then, on the 20th of October 2016, at 28 weeks and six days, I was driving home, simply heading back to pick something up I had forgotten. Such a simple errand, but one that would change our lives forever. Less than 50 metres away from my home, as I approached a corner right by my house I saw a car, a woman clearly not looking up until the last minute and one very large bang. And then dust, slowly floating down, a couple of seconds of shock before the most intense pain I had ever experienced in my life hit me. My entire abdomen was in agony, pains coming and going and suddenly it was all a blur of paramedics, doctors and midwives, steroid injections and people talking about C-Sections. Thankfully the contractions stopped; the quick scan showed no bleeding around baby and a good heart rate and I was told everything was fine, the pain would go and to stop worrying.

But his movements were never the same, and the pain just wouldn't go away, despite being repeatedly told it was in my head and told to stop wasting everyone's time. Being 20, and very new to adulthood never mind motherhood, I didn't know how to advocate for myself so I stayed quiet, trying hard to ignore that nagging feeling and telling myself I was being foolish. Leith was born at 39 weeks, a chubby pink little boy who appeared healthy, confirming what I was told, that I was just being paranoid and silly.

So, life went on, those newborn days, a blur of caring for a tiny baby and an eleven month old, baby groups and swimming lessons taking up most of my days and it was bliss. When Leith was only a few months old I found out I was pregnant with my third little boy and was so focused on pregnancy and motherhood that I didn't spot the fact he didn't open his hands, that he didn't roll or move at all, I was just happy and busy.

It was at his 8 month health visitor appointment when she asked me if he could sit up, and just like that the cold descended as I realised he wasn't even close to being able to, in fact he wasn't even close to rolling or opening his hands like he should have. The health visitor just said to wait until he was 11 months and call her if he couldn't sit by then. I tried my best to quash the cold, hard feeling of panic building in my chest and spent the three months trying everything I could to encourage him to sit. When the 11 month deadline hit, and he still couldn't sit, I called the health visitor to be met with the harsh response of "You should have called the doctors weeks ago," and I just remember feeling like a total failure. I cried myself to sleep that night and called the doctors in the morning. An urgent referral was put through and I was told to wait and not panic too much.

A few weeks later I gave birth to my third little boy, and eleven days later we went up to the hospital to see the consultant. I answered all the questions, told them as much as I could and for the first time asked the fateful question: Is this cerebral palsy from the accident? "No, the accident wasn't that bad and I'm sorry to say we are looking for genetic diseases, all of your children will need to be tested". My world crumbled and the next six months were the darkest of my life. The anticipatory grief was crippling and I sadly have no fond memories of my third child's first few months.

In the August, after 6 months of hell, blood tests galore and an MRI, I went along to our first community paediatrician appointment, no clue what to expect but we had a consultant appointment the following week so I wasn't expecting much. I sat there, babies in their pushchair ready to go through the hundred and one questions you have to go through at the start of every appointment. The doctor, a kind woman, I grew to love while she worked there, looked deep into my eyes and said "The MRI results are in, it is cerebral palsy, all other tests are clear, and yes, I think you should speak to a lawyer about the RTA". I was too shocked to even process that this was good news, there was no flood of relief, just numb shock and a little sadness. The rest of the appointment was her explaining and showing me the results again and again.

I drove home running on autopilot, until a friend called me to discuss a play date, and suddenly the reality that my baby had brain damage and would never walk, never talk (jokes on them, he never stops now) and while I wanted to be relieved it wasn't a degenerative disease, I couldn't. I couldn't feel even the slightest hint of happiness. I cried and cried to my friend, cried and cried for weeks after and that cloud didn't lift for a good few years if I'm honest.

But it did lift, that anger and grief did eventually become background noise and eventually forgotten. Were we gaslighted and ignored? Yes. Do we still get ignored and gaslighted? Yes, but I'm much better at calling them out on it. The fights have never stopped since, from a two year war for an EHCP that actually reflected his needs, to our ongoing fight for a house that he can actually live safely and comfortably in; the fights will never end, I've accepted that. But there are some amazing pockets of joy, some incredible people I wouldn't have met otherwise, and at the centre of all this, the most wonderful, kind intelligent boy you could ever meet.

I'm pleased to tell you that despite their predictions, he doesn't stop talking, he is top of his class for Maths and can read better than his older brother. He cannot walk, he had to have SDR surgery to manage his pain (which so far has been a huge success) and he will have ongoing issues for the rest of his life. But he is wonderful, and that is all that matters.

Our family's journey with Sanfilippo

By Natasha Clarke

Natasha Clarke lives in Nantwich, Cheshire with her husband Jonathan and 3 children, Lucas (19), Isabelle (18) and Lilia (8). Lilia has Sanfilippo type B which is part of a family of conditions called mucopolysaccharide disease. Since Lilia's diagnosis in 2021, Natasha has been trying to spread awareness of this rare condition so that more research can be done to help find a cure and give hope for the children and families affected.

Our family's journey with Sanfilippo

On 9 June 2021, our beautiful daughter, Lilia, was diagnosed with a rare and degenerative illness called MPS IIIB or Sanfilippo Syndrome, Type B. This is our story about the years leading up to her diagnosis and how our lives changed and continues to change post diagnosis.

One of the most challenging parts of this disease is that the children are all born healthy. We had no idea during the pregnancy, after the birth or for the first two years of Lilia's life that she was anything but healthy. She met all her milestones, sitting up, crawling and even walking at 10 months. She started talking and she was interested in everyone and everything.

At around two years, she started to have gastrointestinal problems. She was frequently sick with several bouts of diarrhoea. Initially we put it down to her starting nursery and picking up a lot of bugs. It was only through keeping a diary of her sickness that we realised that it was a reaction towards dairy and soya products and had her referred to a nutritionist who advised us about the dairy and soya ladder. It took us about six months to clear her system out but we found a diet that worked and she got back to good health and going back to nursery which she loved.

We then noticed that she had a slight speech delay which we put down to her being so poorly for the last six months. Lilia would struggle to put a sentence together even though she continued to have good understanding and would carry out instructions and she had a large number of words and phrases. We were referred to speech and language and also audiology to check her hearing. It was at this time that we learned that she had fluid and wax in both ears and surgery was scheduled to remove this and insert grommets. Again, we were hopeful that once these obstacles were fixed the speech would come along. Several people advised me not to worry as she was the baby of the family and would catch up in time and that this was a common problem with glue ears and speech development.

Following the grommets, Lilia's speech did seem to improve. However, the speech and language therapist was not satisfied with her progress and referred her to a paediatrician for further assessment. The paediatrician found that Lilia was easily distracted and slightly delayed but could not find any obvious problems and asked us to come back for a further assessment in six months. It was at that time that Covid hit and all the schools and nurseries were closed. Lilia was 4 and we were worried that she would not be ready to start school as she was still struggling to potty train with consistency. However, we found that she thrived at home, her speech was improving and we were able to have a mini conversation with her. Even though she was behind, we found that she was continuing to learn slowly with patience and consistency. I had a meeting with our local school to warn them that she may need additional help and they were very supportive and said that they would do all that they could.

Lilia started school with all the restrictions that Covid brought and it was then that her development started to plateau and then drop. We noticed that she was saying less than usual and in a couple of months stopped speaking completely. The speech and language therapist at school told us that she thought Lilia had regressive Autism and she said that she would refer us to another paediatrician as the one Lilia was under had left the NHS.

Fortunately, an appointment came through relatively quickly and the paediatrician asked us to do a number of tests. These were urine tests, blood tests, ultrasound and also an MRI. The initial genetic screening had come back negative so we were not too concerned. After 4 months of waiting we were called in to be told that she was one of 150 children in the UK to have MPSIII (Sanfilippo). There are 4 types of Sanfilippo and Lilia is 1 of 44 in the UK to have Sanfilippo Type B. We were told to contact the MPS society in the

UK for advice and support and referred to Manchester Children's hospital where they had specialist consultants for MPS disorders.

The months following diagnosis were a blur of appointments, trying to find out as much as possible to help us navigate through this drastic change of our circumstances. We found out that Sanfilippo is a recessive condition which means that Lilia inherited a non working gene from both parents. Essentially her body is missing a very specific enzyme to break down cellular waste. Because of this, there are no symptoms until the waste starts to build up and cause problems. As the waste continues to build up, the symptoms become more severe. Every cell in the body is affected. Lilia, like other children with the same disease, often share similar mannerisms and physical characteristics. They have thick coarse hair, dark eyebrows and a low nasal bridge. As Sanfilippo progresses it damages every part of her body but particularly her brain. This is why it is sometimes called "childhood dementia" and eventually she will forget how to walk, eat, sit and is not expected to live beyond her teens.

The irony is that if she was diagnosed earlier (before she turned 2) she would have been eligible for gene therapy which is used to help the body manufacture the missing enzyme. She may have also been eligible for a clinical trial to replace the missing enzyme on a regular basis.

Lilia is 8 now and is attending a special needs school near to us. We were very fortunate to get a space there as they are very oversubscribed. She loves attending school and there are nurses, speech and language therapists and physiotherapists on site to manage her symptoms and give us support as needed. The MPS society have also been a huge support to us, giving us advice on disability allowances and adaptations that we have to make in the house. They have also put us in touch with other Sanfilippo families and organised events for us all to meet up so we don't feel alone in this journey.

At the moment Lilia is doing well but she has mild hearing loss, problems with her eyesight, her liver is enlarged and her joints are starting to stiffen. She has trouble sleeping at night and is prescribed melatonin which is sometimes helpful, but many times doesn't seem to work at all.

Even though there are difficult days, there is still a lot of laughter and a cause for joy in the house. Lilia is a very happy little girl who loves going on her trike, being in the water, looking at books, watching her favourite TV shows, eating and spending time with her family.

We have found the love and support of a caring group of people who we call "Our Sanfilippo family" made up of families all over the world going through the same situation. It has been fantastic to be able to reach out to them for support and advice.

Children like Lilia are the most special, bravest and happiest children you will ever meet and their families are the most amazing because of the resilient way in which they live their lives, never giving up and continually living in the present and fighting for a better future.

George's ASD rollercoaster

By Holly Provost

Holly is a 44-year-old mum, part time employee, school parent governor and avid learner of ASD, who lives in Enfield, London with her partner Stephen and their two boys, 7-year-old George and 3-year-old Fred. George has Autism Spectrum Disorder.

George's ASD rollercoaster

I am a twin and ever since we were young, I had always expressed that I did not want children because I couldn't bring up a child on my own and didn't trust the potential child's father to stick around and support us. I had no responsibilities, at least none like that of bringing up a child so enjoyed life to the fullest. I was 38 when I found out I was pregnant with my first child and to be honest I didn't know how to feel. It wasn't on the cards for me, but I knew that I was going to keep this baby even if I did have to do it on my own, but I didn't have to as I'd met an amazing man, Stephen. My pregnancy was not easy; I suffered with Symphysis Pubis Dysfunction (SPD) causing pain with mobility and I had Gestational Diabetes that had to be controlled with insulin injections 4 times a day. Our scans had all gone well, and our child's predicted birth date was 18th January 2017, a day before my birthday and 2 days before Stephen's so with that in mind we decided to not find out the gender of our child rather it be a surprise birthday gift for us both. At the end of December 2016, we attended hospital for an appointment and the doctor said that our child would likely be big due to my medical issues so wanted to book us in at an earlier date for baby's birth, so we agreed 04th January 2017.

Between 04th and 08th January we had brought on labour that had to be reversed for risk of a collapsed uterus, a potential blood clot in my leg due to swelling from an injection, an epidural to break my waters as my cervix was too scarred from pre-cancer cells being removed in my 20's that I couldn't dilate. When everything finally seemed to be going in the right direction, the consultant came to examine me only to find the umbilical cord had prolapsed so it was down to theatre for an emergency c-section. On 8th January 2017 at 15:09, weighing 6lb 4oz, our beautiful little boy George was born.

When George was a baby, we regularly attended weigh ins and his development was very consistent being on or around the 50th centile and reaching all the expected benchmarks. We only ever attended a couple of baby groups due to a bad experience when attending a 6-week course I'd booked myself onto so I preferred to meet friends whose babies were a similar age to George for play dates. We struggled with family support due to myself and Stephen's parents being elderly and not living local to us and so the only real family support we had was my twin and my best friend who were always on the end of the phone if needed but were both in full time employment with families of their own. By the time George reached the age of around 2, we knew something wasn't right. It seemed like literally over night he had gone from saying a few words, Mumma, Dadda, cat, etc and engaging with us to the complete opposite. He stopped talking, would walk on his toes, flap his hands, and struggle with eye contact. He would lay for hours on the floor with a car just watching the wheels going round, he visibly struggled in noisy situations and stopped wanting to engage with little people. We asked our health visitor to come and see us, she had always been amazing, and we spoke to her about our concerns. The memory of that day isn't clear but I do remember her asking questions about George's development for an assessment she was doing and at the end she told us he was scoring much lower on the scale than he should and so she would set us on the path for assessment.

In September 2020, George started nursery at a local Primary School. Stephen had gone to this school as a child, and it was recommended to us by our health visitor as having good support for children who were neurodiverse, but it was still a mainstream school. From the onset, the support we received from the school, staff, and particularly the school SENCO was remarkable and quite frankly I am not sure where we would be now without them. She made sure that any difficulties or challenges George had were documented to begin compiling evidence to support an EHCP which we knew he would need. Also because George was non-verbal, it was suggested we consider a SEN school to better support his needs, and this documentation would support our case. Then Covid hit and I was pregnant with my second child. Lockdown was cruel to many people and families, and we saw first-hand the devastation it caused as Stephen is a funeral director but for George it was a turning point. With visual aids and strategies given to us, I worked tirelessly with George to try and move his development along, spending every day with him, talking, playing, watching, and desperately trying to understand his world of which I knew nothing about. George was also having Speech and Language Therapy in the form of playful communication. Our therapist was incredible teaching me strategies to support George and help us to engage with each other on a level that worked for George. In February 2021, and after we had finished our playful communication therapy, George was assessed by the SaLT team and the nursery manager who both wrote what their findings and opinions of George were. Then in March 2021 we attended an online paediatrician appointment. At the end of this assessment, it was confirmed George had a diagnosis of Autism Spectrum Disorder (ASD). I thanked the paediatrician for her time, put the phone down and sobbed. I cried for the child I felt I had lost, for the diagnosis, for the uncertainty of what was to come and for what the future would hold for George. Up until this point, other than the school and SaLT the support had been minimal. Once the diagnosis came, so did the support, but it was very over whelming as so many people and organisations reached out; it was difficult to know who to engage with first. I attended workshop after workshop learning about behaviour, eating habits, toilet training and was sent through more visual aids from the local authority Autism team. We had no diagnosis of Autism in mine or Stephen's family until this point so trying to learn about the diagnosis and then teach friends and relatives was incredibly difficult especially with the older generation in our families who just didn't get it. I was frustrated and angry with those who didn't understand that George needed routine, he struggled with change, was sensitive to sounds, smells, colours, and textures and that to understand George you needed to immerse yourself into George's world where he would need to regulate himself and stimulate himself but more importantly, he wasn't a naughty child - he was an Autistic child.

When George returned to school in September 2021, the SENCO met us and asked if we had considered a SEN school while we had been off. Before I could answer, George spoke a sentence. You could see she was shocked and thrilled and from this moment she has done everything in her power to make sure George gets the support he needs. She has worked with many children over the years who have special needs and bares the scars to prove her resilience and her phenomenal ability to adapt herself to a multitude of different people, not forgetting that she also supports deaf children with BSL classes.

Our life so far has been a rollercoaster. In George's earlier years he suffered regular eye infections, ear infections, tonsilitis, night terrors, raging temperatures and long stays in hospital with pneumonia and now has molar and incisor hyper mineralisation of his teeth meaning the enamel is weak and causes crumbling of his teeth and sensitivity which will need regular treatment and check-ups. He has always struggled with co-ordination, bumping into things, and falling over. The worst was when he had to have his head glued after falling headfirst into the edge of a windowsill. Then there was the time we had a new front door fitted that could only be accessed by a key. Stephen went to put rubbish out and George shut him out. He had to break a window to get in. We had the lock changed to a thumb turn style lock and in April 2022 George was able to climb over a baby gate at the top of the stairs, take the chain off the door, open the front door, and left the house. It was 2am, freezing cold and he was in just a pair of pj's. He was seen by a passer by who called the police. His speech wasn't great, and he couldn't tell them where he had come from only that daddy had a camper van. At around 3:30am, and amazing investigation work by the police, they called Stephen and asked us to check his room. He was gone and I was devastated. I had completely underestimated what he was capable of but thankfully he was returned home safe. Needless to say, we now have multiple locks on our front door and an alarm that tells us if the front door is opened. Again, the school were our rock, there was no judgement just concern for all of us and support given. George's EHCP was another challenge as the original was not fit for George's needs so with the help of

SEN Specialist Advocacy Services (an independent SEN Advocacy service for SEN parents) we managed to get everything George needed. I first met Sunil from SENSAS at an EHCP workshop where he gave free advice on EHCPs and making sure they were fit for purpose. I never thought we would need him but when the first draft came and was inadequate, I knew he would be able to help. He had worked in multiple roles within local authorities and was a wealth of knowledge with EHCPs and the law surrounding them. He is now using all his experience and knowledge to support other SEN parents secure their EHC plan rights. We got to within days of our tribunal date and the Local Authority conceded. His service was not free but was the best money I'd ever spent, and he was worth every penny. Having said all of this, I love this rollercoaster we are on. George has motivated me to understand every bit of his world with reading books, scrolling websites, doing educational courses, and talking with people who are in a similar situation to us. He has taught me patience, that this journey is not a sprint but a very laid-back marathon, that he is unique, and I should never, ever underestimate what he is capable of. I can't make him do anything he doesn't want to do but with visual aids, preparation and support, things like the dentist are usually meltdown free now. We are always learning, and no day is the same. His world is complex and sometimes I just sit and watch him, how he navigates different situations, wondering how he sees life and the wonderful people around him, apprehensive but excited for his future. I don't understand his world, but I will spend the rest of my life trying to find out with George's help.

Nenna's Song – A fairytale in three parts.

By Paul Arvidson

Paul Arvidson is a carer for a teenaged girl with a CTBP1 mutation. This condition is so rare that there's only twelve kids in the world with it. He lives in Somerset with his wife and one more teenaged daughter. In order to remain sane when he gave up work, Paul took up writing. So far he's written a Sci-Fi Epic with blind Space Guinea Pigs and a Thriller starring a Sweary Teen in a Wheelchair. He's also featured in the poetry collection 'Helix of Love' Produced by Brighton and Sussex Uni, Published by Wellcome Trust. If you liked it, you can find more of his work at: www.paularvidson.co.uk

Nenna's Song – A fairytale in three parts.

1

There was a tap at the door. John put down his coffee. The usual early morning pre-school noise filled the house, the kids being harassed to their school bags by Jane. He shook his head. Another tap. Not a knock, or a ring on the expensive Google-enabled security bell he'd installed, a tap. A third tap, more insistent this time. He stood and shuffled to the front door. Opening it, he looked left and right into the suburban morning street: nothing. More kids stumbling to school chased/accompanied/frog marched by parents, but no-one at the door.

Kaaarrr!

Startled, John looked down. At his feet was an enormous black bird, the colour and shape of a crow but the size of a cat. Was it a raven? John had never been to the Tower of London and had never concentrated at school and now regretted both. The bird held a white envelope in its beak. John stared down, perplexed. The bird cocked its head to one side and regarded him with one shiny black eye. It dropped the letter on the doorstep. He glared at it, then at the bird. The bird tapped the see-through window where the address should be. John looked. There was neat typeface in the window, it read: *John and Jane.* No surname. No address. Perhaps you didn't need an address if you were getting a crow to deliver your post. What was he thinking? He was clearly losing his mind.

Kaaarrr!

The bird tapped the envelope again impatiently and John picked it up. His mystery postal worker hopped backwards, watching him beadily.

"What?" John held the envelope out. The bird cocked his head towards the letter. "I need to open it?" There was clearly not enough coffee in the world for him to be conversing with crows this early in the morning. He shook his head and opened the flap. After a header from: The Department of Important Scientific Information and a date, a 'To:' line that just read 'John and Jane', in the middle of the page were just four words:

Your Child Is Special

He opened his mouth. Closed it again and was just about to ask the bird, before he realized that, with a flap, it had taken to the air.

Ka-aarr! it said and flew off over the houses.

John turned to go back in, but instead of the cream double glazed door he'd come out of, there was a floor length velvet curtain, in a deep purple. Since it was still the only way back into the house, open mouthed, he pushed through the curtain.

2

The house was extreme. Everything seemed garish. Like a new TV with the colour setting up too high. Everything was noisier, just like adverts: more of everything. Even the smells were louder, the dog, the recycling, the anti-septic spray.

"Don't forget, it's your turn to walk the youngest to school," called Jane from the kitchen.

He followed Jane's voice. When he got to the kitchen, he saw it. His youngest child was glowing.

"You okay, love?" Jane was stuffing the last of the school stuff into the youngest's bag.

John nodded. As soon as Janes's gaze was off him, he looked round the room. The eldest was ready and on their way out the door: not glowing. Jane, not glowing. He looked down at his own hands just to double check. Also, not glowing. Just the youngest.

"She's had all her meds, you've got five minutes to finish your coffee, I'm off to work, see you tonight," said Jane and moved towards the door, shouldering a canvas bag as she went. "You good?" She looked him in the eyes.

John forced as convincing a smile as he could'., "Yeah." He gave her a brief kiss and she was gone. Then with a 'bye Dad', the eldest was gone too. He turned to the youngest. "You good to walk today?" Her chair sat in the hall, though whether she needed it or not depended on how she felt on the day. She nodded. "Let's go!" She looked up at him, smiling. Though she never spoke, she always made her feelings clear.

Outside was no less intense. The sky was too blue, the birds sounded nearly hysterical, and the traffic rumbling from everywhere shook John's insides. At the end of the path, though, hand in hand with his daughter, things got really odd. No-one would look him in the eye. Here he was, on his everyday school run, with his—granted—glowing child, but still… His next-door neighbour was on her way to school in the opposite direction with her son. He offered a cheery greeting, but she put her head down and hurried on. John looked up and down the road. Everyone on school runs. But here was the thing: there were more glowing people. Not everyone, not many, maybe one in five? He shook his head to focus. Mrs Jones from three doors down was picking a crisp packet off the path with her grabber to avoid bending and carefully putting it in a wheelie bin. She was glowing.

"Morning!" said John.

"Hi loves," she said back cheerfully.

Not everyone was ignoring them then.

The school was only two blocks away, but all the way there, John couldn't help but notice the glowing people: a woman in a car, an old guy on a mobility scooter; for every four people, give or take, there was a fifth one with a halo round them. Standing in the queue waiting for the doors to open, John shifted from foot to foot uneasily. His daughter tugged his arm and pointed at her non-glowing friend with her mum across the small schoolyard. John nodded and let her go. As he looked up, he noticed that a group of mums to his left, whom he vaguely knew, looked away when he caught their gaze. Then he heard the muttering: "So brave,", "What a hero,", "I'd never manage..." He realized with some degree of surprise, and not a little horror, that they were talking about him.

Before he could say anything, the door opened and the smiling, non-glowing face of Miss Simpkins met them. She stood back from the door to let parents and children into the hallway where coats and bags were stowed, delivering a few words to each pair as they came in. When John passed through, she smiled beatifically at the two of them and said, "Well done!" He stopped, mouth open, but quickly got roped into coat pegs and checking sandwiches and pencils and kisses on the head, then, looking up, the small hall was empty and the classroom was full. He stood slowly. Instead of the door he'd come in through, was the purple curtain.

On the other side of this curtain was darkness, stillness, and silence. There was a floor. That was all he could tell, he placed his hand out palm forwards in front of him, like some weird martial arts stance. When there was nothing directly in front of him, he shuffled slowly forwards in the dark, saying, "Hello? Hello?" There didn't even seem to be any walls for the sound to echo off; the darkness sucked his voice away. It made him feel awkward, so he stopped calling. Other than the noise of his feet on the floor, there was total silence.

CLICK!

A cone of light, from somewhere in the roof. On the floor at its base, a leather chair, a swanky office style thing. Nothing else showed up in the space. Just the chair and the light above it. John blinked to adjust his vision. With nothing else to do, he shuffled towards the chair. It smelled reassuringly of real leather. He sat in it.

"Welcome! Welcome to The Rest of Your Life!" The booming voice came from everywhere at once. It was a professional presenter voice. An older man's voice that should have either been selling cars or presenting game shows.

John: "Hello?"

Host: "Hello John, and welcome! Why don't you tell us a little bit about yourself?"

John: "Err, I'm John, I'm 46, married to Jane, I've got two kids—"
Host: "And what exactly is it you do for a living?"

John: "Well, I err... I used to—"

Host: "Don't need to know about the past, we'd be here all night—"

From everywhere at once there echoed canned laughter. It cut off like someone had thrown a switch.

Host: "What do you do now?"

John: "Well, I... I'm a carer?"

Host: "And do you find that a *rewarding* career? You're certainly not doing it for the money!" [Laughter]

John: "Its... err... well, it's not really a career."

Host: "No, you're right, it is *not*. Let's hope you have as much luck with all of the questions tonight."

John: "What questions?"

Host: "Round One! About your child. First question: what was the exact weight of your child the last time they were weighed?"

John: "Err... I think it was thirty-six kilos-ish?"

Host: "No, the correct answer is 36.4 Kgs. Next question: what is the exact name of the condition that your child has?"

John: "Oh, I know this—CTBP1."

Host: "No, that's the name of the gene that causes the condition... the name of the condition is...?"

John: "Oh, 'H' something— Err... H-A-D-D-S! That's it HADDS!"

Host: "Close, but not close enough, your child in fact has: HADDTS. Different syndrome entirely."

John: "What?"

Host: "Okay, an easy one for two points. What are the symptoms of HADDTS?"

John: "Err, Hypotonia, Ataxia, Developmental Delay and—"

Host: "I'll have to hurry you..."

John: "I... err... I don't know!"

Host: "Tooth Enamel Defects."

John: "What? She doesn't have those."

Host: "I'm sorry, we have to take what it says on the card."

John: "This is—"

John was cut off abruptly by a loud beeping.

Host: "And that's the end of round one. John, you've scored a total of one point." [Applause] "Okay. It's all to play for here, now it's the Quick-Fire Round. First question: Do you feel guilty?"

John: "What?"

Host: "Simple question, John. Yes or no answer. Do you feel guilty?"

John: "Well, sometimes?"
Host: "No, what's on the card, I'm afraid. The answer is 'YES, all the time.' Next: Do you feel like you're the worst friend ever?"

John: "Err..."

Host: "Have to press you—"

John: "Yes!"

Host: "Correct answer! Well done. You do in fact feel like you're the worst friend ever, because you hardly go out and you're always cancelling things last minute. That's your second point. Okay next: do you feel entitled to any help for your child, monetary or otherwise?"

John: "No."

Host: "Well done, that's your third point. It was a bit of an easy one as you're made to feel this way by society and by the lack of resource the government allots. But any point's a point right?" [Laughter] "Okay, next question: will there ever be a cure for your daughter?"

John: "No."

Host: "That isn't entirely right; I'm going to give you half a point for that. The correct answer is 'nobody really knows'."

John: "Wait up! I thought you said these are yes or no answers?"

Host: "I'm sorry, the judge's word is final. Next: Do you feel like a failing parent?"

John: "Hey, that's not a fair question—"

Host: "Life's not fair, John, you of all people should know that. The answer was 'Yes, you do feel like a failing parent. All the time.'"

John: "This quiz is stupid. Stop now."

Host: "Afraid we can't stop while there's time on the clock. Next question: when was the last time you made love with your wife?"

John: "That's it. I'm out of here—"

John got up, then heard the sound of an audience booing. It got louder, which was just as well, as he didn't really want to hear the answer to the question. He blundered out of the chair, leaving it spinning in the light, and stumbled off into the darkness. In ten metres, he couldn't see in front of himself again. He risked a quick look behind him, but there was nothing there now: no chair, no light, no phantom audience. Backing away, he felt the curtain again behind him. He breathed a huge sigh of relief and pushed through. He was back in the hall of his home.

"Don't forget, it's your turn to walk the youngest to school," called Jane from the kitchen.

John screamed.

Final words

I would once again like to express my thanks and gratitude to all the parents who have bravely shared their stories. Although each story is so different, and despite the challenges, there is one thing that stands out – the immense love that these parents have for their children. These children are remarkable and so are the parents, but there is so much that could be done to make life a little easier, and the system a little fairer.

What happens to those families who do not have the ability or strength to fight the system? Also, some services are only available privately, so children in low-income families may be excluded.

One underlying theme in the book is 'Who is caring for the carers?' It does seem that the care, support, and education provided is a postcode lottery and parents always have to fight to get the resources they need.

I hope that this book has given you an insight into the highs and lows of navigating this different path, with very little guidance or signposting. The greatest support most parents have found has been in fellow parents on a similar journey. We need to support each other and know that we are not alone. Please share this book far and wide with anyone who finds themselves on this special parenting journey, or with professionals that work with these amazing families.

If you would like to connect with the authors, you can find us in the facebook group 'Parenting on a different path.' If you also have a story to share, please contact me in the group, or email parentingonadifferentpath@gmail.com. I would welcome stories from all diversities and communities.

Glossary

AAC – An Augmentative and Alternative Device: a tablet or laptop that helps someone with speech or language impairment to communicate.

ADD – Attention Deficit Disorder

ADHD – Attention Deficit Hyperactivity Disorder

ASD – Autism Spectrum Disorder

AuDHD – A combination of Autism and ADHD

BSL – British Sign Language

CAMHS – Child and Adolescent Mental Health Services

CICU – Cardiac Intensive Care Unit

CP – Cerebral Palsy

DLA – Disability Living Allowance

DOLS – Deprivation of Liberty Safeguards

EHCP – Education Health and Care Plan

FDA review – Food and Drug Administration

ICU – Intensive Care Unit

Makaton – A visual way to develop communication skills, which help stimulate sounds and words.

MRI – Magnetic Resonance Imaging: A non invasive medical imaging test that produces detailed images of the internal structure of the human body.

NG tube – Nasogastric (nose to stomach) tube that is used for temporary medical problems

NICU – Neonatal Intensive Care Unit: Babies who are born early, have health problems or a difficult birth go here for 24 hour care

OT – Occupational Therapist

PECS – Picture Exchange Communication System: An approach that develops expressive communication skills using pictures

PICU – Paediatric Intensive Care Unit

PMLD – Profound and multiple learning difficulties

RESUS - Resuscitation

SALT – Speech and Language Therapy

SCBU – Special Care Baby Unit

SEN/SEND – Special Educational Needs/Special Educational Needs and Disabilities

Social Prescriber – Someone who connects people to activities, groups and services in their community in order to support health and wellbeing

SUDEP – Sudden Unexpected Death in Epilepsy

Support directory

The following contacts have been mentioned by authors as a valuable resource and they have not been involved in the authorship of the stories or poems.

National / International

Action Duchenne - https://www.actionduchenne.org
Contact: info@actionduchenne.org

Arfid Awareness UK - https://www.arfidawarenessuk.org
Contact: info@arfidawarenessuk.org

BACP (Counselling changes lives) – https://www.bacp.co.uk
Contact: bacp@bacp.co.uk

Brainwave - https://www.brainwave.org.uk
Contact: enquiries@brainwave.org.uk

British Dyslexia Association - https://www.bdadyslexia.org.uk
Contact: There is a form on the website to use

CAMHS – https://www.nhs.uk/mental-health/children-and-young-adults/mental-health-support/mental-health-services/
Contact: referral from a professional

Cerebra – https://cerebra.org.uk
Contact: enquiries@cerebra.org.uk

Contact for families with disabled children - https://contact.org.uk
Contact: info@contact.org.uk

Council for Disabled Children – https://councilfordisabledchildren.org.uk
Contact: enquiries@ncb.org.uk

Dame Vera Lynn Childrens Charity - https://dvlcc.org.uk
Contact: info@dvlcc.org.uk

Define Fine - https://www.definefine.org.uk
Contact: There is a form on the website to use

Disability Grants - https://www.disability-grants.org
Contact: contact@disability-grants.org

Duchenne Family Support Group - https://dfsg.org.uk
Contact: info@dfsg.org.uk

Duchenne Registry - https://www.duchenneregistry.org
Contact: coordinator@duchenneregistry.org

Duchenne UK - https://www.duchenneuk.org
Contact: There is a form on the website to use

Home Start - https://www.home-start.org.uk
Contact: info@home-start.org.uk

IPSEA (SEND Law leading charity) – https://www.ipsea.org.uk
Contact: Various means available on the website

Kids (Disabled children say we can) – https://www.kids.org.uk
Contact: There is a form on the website to use

Mencap – https://www.mencap.org.uk
Contact: Various means available on the website

National Deaf Children's Society – https://www.ndcs.org.uk
Contact: ndcs@ndcs.org.uk

Newlife Charity – https://newlifecharity.co.uk
Contact: There is a form on the website to use

Parent Project Muscular Dystrophy – https://www.parentprojectmd.org
Contact: info@parentprojectmd.org

Pitt Hopkins Syndrome UK – https://pitthopkins.org.uk
Contact: sue@pitthopkins.org.uk

Positive about Down Syndrome – https://positiveaboutdownsyndrome.co.uk
Contact: info@downsyndromeuk.co.uk

Scope – https://www.scope.org.uk
Contact: Various means available on the website

Selective Mutism – https://www.selectivemutism.org.uk
Contact: There is a form on the website to use

SEN SAS Advocacy (Specialist Advocacy Services) – www.sensasadvocacy.co.uk
Contact: contact@sensasadvocacy.co.uk

SENsational Life – http://www.sensational-life.com
Contact: info@sensational-life.com

SOS SEN – https://sossen.org.uk
Contact: There is a form on the website to use

Spinal Muscular Atrophy UK – https://smauk.org.uk
Contact: office@smauk.org.uk

SWAN UK (Part of Genetic Alliance UK) – https://geneticalliance.org.uk
Contact: info@undiagnosed.org.uk

The Cerebral Visual Impairment Society – https://cvisociety.org.uk
Contact: info@cvisociety.org.uk

Your Elementz (Counselling for parent carers) – https://www.yourelementz.com
Contact: There is a form on the website to use

Local

ADHD Solutions (Leicestershire) - https://www.adhdsolutions.org
Contact: info@adhdsolutions.org

Bamboozle Theatre (Leicestershire) - https://bamboozletheatre.co.uk
Contact: info@bamboozletheatre.co.uk

Camp Charnwood (Leicestershire) - https://www.campcharnwood.co.uk
Contact: info@campcharnwood.co.uk

Carers Centre (Leicestershire and Rutland) https://www.claspthecarerscentre.org.uk
Contact: enquiries@thecarerscentre.org.uk

Downright Special (Hull) - https://downrightspecial.co.uk
Contact: enquiries@downrightspecial.co.uk

Facebook – Charnwood Neurodiverse Families Parent Support Group
https://www.facebook.com/groups/1110843446282788

Facebook – Spectrum Autism Group (Market Harborough)
https://www.facebook.com/groups/spectrumautismgroup

FTM Dance (Leicestershire & Nottinghamshire) - https://ftmdance.co.uk
Contact: referrals@ftmdance.co.uk

Leicestershire SEND Hub - https://www.leicestershiresendhub.org.uk
Contact: admin@leicestershiresendhub.org.uk

Menphys (Leicestershire and Rutland) - https://menphys.org.uk
Contact: info@menphys.org.uk

Miracles To Believe In (Leicestershire) - https://mtbi.co.uk
Contact: aysherox49@btinternet.com

Mosaic 1898 (Leicestershire) - https://www.mosaic1898.co.uk
Contact: enquiries@mosaic1898.co.uk

Mum Stop (Leicestershire) - https://www.mumstop.co.uk
Contact: There is a form on the website to use

NHS Cambridge University Hospitals -
https://www.cuh.nhs.uk/our-people/neurodiversity-at-cuh
Contact: There is a form on the website to use

Rainbows (East Midlands) - https://www.rainbows.co.uk
Contact: administration@rainbows.co.uk

Ruby's Fund (Cheshire) - https://www.rubysfund.co.uk
Contact: info@rubysfund.co.uk

Vista (Leicestershire) - https://www.vistablind.org.uk
Contact: info@vistablind.org.uk

Zoe's Place (Coventry / Liverpool / Middlesborough) - https://www.zoes-place.org.uk
Contact: headoffice@zoes-place.org.uk

Other resources

A Grief That Never Ends: Chronic Sorrow
https://www.psychologytoday.com/intl/blog/navigating-the-serpentine-path/202212/a-grief-that-never-ends-chronic-sorrow

Epilepsy Action – Infantile epileptic spasms syndrome information
https://www.epilepsy.org.uk/info/syndromes/west-syndrome-infantile-spasms

Great Ormond Street Hospital - Periventricular leukomalacia information
https://www.gosh.nhs.uk/conditions-and-treatments/conditions-we-treat/periventricular-leukomalacia

RNIB – Cerebral visual impairment and PMLD information
https://www.rnib.org.uk/professionals/health-social-care-education-professionals/education-professionals/cerebral-visual-impairment-and-pmld

Scope - Periventricular leukomalacia information
https://www.scope.org.uk/advice-and-support/periventricular-leukomalacia

Printed in Great Britain
by Amazon